G.O.L.D.

God Overcomes Loss from Death

Cinny Roy
Tambra Breyer
Patsy Andow-Plum
Kathy D. Schibler

Copyright © 2020 by Cinny Roy, Tambra Breyer, Patsy Andow-Plum, Kathy D. Schibler. All rights reserved.

This book or any portion thereof may not be reproduced or used in any manner whatsoever without the express written permission of the publisher except for the use of brief quotations in a scholarly work or book review. For permissions or further information contact Braughler Books LLC at:

   info@braughlerbooks.com

Cover photo: photoBeard/Shutterstock.com

Printed in the United States of America
Published by Braughler Books LLC., Springboro, Ohio

First printing, 2020

ISBN: 978-1-970063-56-1

Library of Congress Control Number: 2020905034

Ordering information: Special discounts are available on quantity purchases by bookstores, corporations, associations, and others. For details, contact the publisher at:

   sales@braughlerbooks.com

   or at 937-58-BOOKS

For questions or comments about this book, please write to:

   info@braughlerbooks.com

DEDICATION

This workbook is the culmination of three years of research, writing, tears, prayers and laughter. We dedicate this to our loved ones who have left us behind. It is because of our unending love for them that we present this work of our hearts to you in hopes it will soothe your soul at this difficult time. God and God alone, equipped us for such a time as this speaking great insight and wisdom as we wrote, edited and refined the lessons. He is our glory - God is the Overcomer of Loss from Death.

Contents

CHAPTER 1
Introduction To Grief - The Broken Bowl 1

CHAPTER 2
Unique Grief - My Broken Bowl, My Broken Life 13

CHAPTER 3
Emotions - My Shattered Bowl. 27

CHAPTER 4
Why - Why Did My Bowl Break 37

CHAPTER 5
Life Losses - Broken Pieces in My Bowl 53

CHAPTER 6
Stuck In Grief - My Pieces Can't Go Back the Same Way . . . 61

CHAPTER 7
Change Direction - Seeing a New Wholeness of My Bowl . . . 79

CHAPTER 8
Integrating Loss - Glue of Recovery 95

CHAPTER 9
Transformation - Gold Glue. 107

CHAPTER 10
Something To Celebrate - In the Artist's Gallery of Life 121

References 125
Appendix A: Resources........................... 128
Appendix B: G.O.L.D. Scriptures 131
About the Authors 135

CHAPTER 1
Introduction To Grief
The Broken Bowl

I am forgotten as though I were dead; I have become like broken pottery. Psalm 31:12

G.O.L.D. — God Overcomes Loss from Death. Since Creation, God has been about your redemption. He has been about the preservation and recovery of you from danger and loss. This workbook gives you the opportunity to express the pain you have surrounding the death of someone you love. Along the way, you will begin to recover and experience God's glory as He draws you to Him.

PRAY: O Father, as your child, I come to you for help. Calm my heart. Enable me to see what I need to see. Make me aware of my need for healing and show me Your truth. Bring to my mind the buried pain. Surface any hidden hurt and the exact circumstances that caused it. I ask You to help my wounded heart to heal. I know that You have the power to make me whole. I am willing to face whatever You want me to face so that I can love and remember freely with joy. In Your holy name I pray. Amen

INTRODUCTION

Kintsukuroi (*keen-tsoo-koo-roy*) is the Japanese art of repairing broken pottery with lacquer dusted or mixed with powdered gold, silver, or platinum. As a philosophy, it treats breakage and repair as part of the history of an object, rather than something to disguise.

When a potter makes a bowl, he forms it by hand with clay. The bowl is formed to the potter's liking, then fired to several thousand degrees and, once finished, presented as a work of art created for a specific purpose.

Imagine if something suddenly happens and the bowl is broken into pieces. You then have a choice to make. You can try to keep the broken pieces hidden, hoping nobody remembers the damage. You can try to repair the item using your own abilities. This will put the bowl back together, but it will always bear the painful reminder of the damage. Or you can repair the bowl in such a manner that it is not only put back together, but it is more beautiful because of how it now reflects its entire history. The bowl can become more beautiful for having been broken. This is Kintsukuroi.

In reading and responding to the material in this workbook, you will experience kintsukuroi of your heart and spirit by taking your broken life vessel and placing it into the Potter's hand.

*Yet you, Lord, are our Father. We are the clay, you are the **potter**; we are all the work of your hand. Isaiah 64:8*

Why Are You Here?

What is your purpose for doing this workbook? There may be something you want or need. Take a moment right now and write your goal on an index card. When you are finished, put it in an envelope, seal it, put your name and today's date on it.

If you are part of a group, hand the envelope to the leaders to keep so they can return it to you towards the end of group.

If you are healing through this workbook on your own, keep the envelope to review when you have finished. We also suggest that you choose a companion to walk through this with you: someone who listens well and protects your confidentiality. Someone who will encourage your healing as you go through these exercises chapter by chapter. This is suggested because some of your thoughts and experiences are learned best when spoken out loud. You "hear" yourself and gain new awareness which leads to healing change.

Misconceptions

There are many misconceptions surrounding grief. Things said to you are meant to help you "get through" the grief. At times they only make you feel more intense emotions, feel like a failure, or feel like you are grieving wrong. Grief may happen because of what you tell yourself.

REFLECT: Circle the incorrect beliefs from the following list that I believe/have believed or have been said about myself:

- Grief shouldn't last too long
- I shouldn't be angry at my loved one/s who died
- Self-control is how I will get through this
- Crying means I am a weak person
- I should be back to normal by now
- I must be strong for others
- I should act distressed even though I am relieved that the person has died
- As a Christian, I should always be joyful
- I should reply "I'm fine," when friends and family ask how I'm doing
- If I feel like I am going crazy, it's due to something other than the loss
- My loved one wouldn't want me to be sad

- Taking time off from prayer groups or church means I am unfaithful to God
- I need to "take on" the good traits of my loved one and be more like them
- I have to do this alone
- I don't want to burden others with my grief
- Somehow I must have been part of why my loved one died
- Other_____

This list begins looking at where distortions about your loss begin. In future chapters, this workbook will discuss some of these misconceptions and how they may prevent you from grieving well.

WHAT IS GRIEF?

- Grief is the normal and natural emotional reaction to loss or change of any kind
- Grief is neither a pathological condition nor a personality disorder (Friedman, 2013)
- Grief can stir up a wide range of emotions caused by the end of or change in a familiar pattern of behavior
- Grief is the normal process of reacting to a loss. The loss may be physical (such as a death), social (such as divorce), or occupational (such as a job)
- Grief emotional reactions can include anger, guilt, anxiety, sadness, and despair
- Grief physical reactions can include sleeping problems, changes in appetite, physical problems, or illness. (WebMD, 2016)

Types of Grief

The following are three types of grief. There will be more discussion provided on some of these later in the workbook.

Anticipatory grief: A reaction to an upcoming, impending, or expected loss event. It can be an important part of the grieving process and can help a person sort out emotions in preparation for the loss. Remember, everyone grieves differently, and anticipatory grief may not necessarily lessen grief or shorten the grieving process. (Conrad Stoppler, 2011)

Complicated grief: For some people, acute grief can gain a foothold and become a chronic, debilitating mental health condition that worsens over time, rather than getting better. This is called complicated grief. Pre-existing mental health conditions, multiple stressors, emotional dependency, or substance abuse issues complicate the grieving process and increase the likelihood of a complicated bereavement disorder that may necessitate professional treatment. (Khoshaba, 2013)

Unresolved grief: There is no definite point in time or a list of symptoms that define this. Unresolved grief lasts longer than usual for a person's social circle or cultural background. It may also be used to describe grief that does not go away or interferes with the person's ability to take care of daily responsibilities. (WebMD, n.d.) This grief is often invisible to the "outside" eye and may necessitate professional treatment.

REFLECT: Which category of grief am I experiencing? Make a note here.

WHAT IS MOURNING AND HOW IS IT DIFFERENT THAN GRIEF?

- Mourning is the outward expression of your grief
- Mourning usually involves culturally determined rituals that help the bereaved person make sense of the end of their loved one's life and give structure to what can feel like a very confusing time
- Mourning can be influenced by personal, familial, cultural, religious, and societal beliefs and customs. Everything from how families prepare themselves and their loved ones for death, how they understand and react to the passing, to the practices for preserving memories of the deceased, their funeral/memorial, burial/cremation, or other ways of handling the remains of the deceased (Khoshaba, 2013)
- Mourning is the process of working through your painful sorrow following a significant loss
- Mourning evokes compassion and expressions of comfort from others
- Mourning in English is sometimes translated from the Greek *klaio*, which means "to wail" (WebMD, n.d.)

Grief is the <u>internal</u> thoughts and feelings you have. "It holds your thoughts, feelings, and images of your experience when someone you love dies. In other words, grief is the internal meaning given to the experience of loss. **Mourning** is when you take the grief you have on the inside and express it <u>outside</u> of yourself. Another way of defining mourning is "grief gone public" or "the outward expression of grief." There is not a right or single way to mourn. Talking about the person who died, crying, expressing your thoughts and feelings through art or music, journaling, praying, and celebrating special anniversary dates that held meaning for the person who died are just a few examples of mourning." (Wolfelt, 2016)

REFLECT: Have I had the opportunity to mourn?

- When

- Where

- How

- Write out my experiences

SADNESS AND DEPRESSION

Culture uses the term "depression" to express any bad and/or poor feelings. Yet there is a difference between sadness and true depression.

Sadness

- Sadness is a normal human emotion often triggered by the loss of a loved one or by other challenging and/or difficult situations
- You feel sad *about* something. When you are adjusting to the loss, your sadness diminishes with time
- You may overreact to normal feelings of sadness and think it is depression
- Depression tends to be associated with its primary symptom of pervasive sadness (sadness that permeates or affects everything)
- Sadness has an identifiable source

Depression

- Many symptoms of depression are experienced as part of the grief process, especially in the early phases of grief
- Depression as a medical diagnosis is an illness. It colors all aspects of your life and has identifiable symptoms. The severity of symptoms may vary from one person to another and these symptoms last longer than two weeks of continual duration
- If someone has had a history of clinical depression, the experience of grief may trigger a recurrence
- Depression "just is" — it does not have an obvious source

If you are feeling sad or depressed, DO speak with someone to "check yourself." Pay attention if friends and family express concern for you. If you are experiencing ongoing depression, please seek professional help for care and treatment.

RESPONSES TO LOSS

Your heart has broken immensely over the loss/es you have experienced. Intense grief touches every part of your life causing you to plummet emotionally, relationally, physically, perceptually, and spiritually, shattering your entire existence.

The effects of this intense grief will vary in degree, ranging from mild to severe, depending on where you are in the grieving process. While you will not experience all the effects, everyone will experience some of them. Realize that these effects are common to everyone who grieves and are temporary...as long as you face the pain of your loss and work through the grief. (Hunt, 2013)

REFLECT: Circle the ones I am experiencing now or have experienced:

Emotional

Grief is an overwhelming emotional reaction/response to loss
Some feelings triggered by grief:

Sorrow	Anguish	Despair	Anger
Resentment	Guilt	Regret	Emptiness
Loneliness	Numbness	Disbelief	Anxiety
Yearning	Love	Appreciation	Envy

- Threat of suicide/self-harm
- I don't feel anything which can be awkward since there "should" be a sense of loss
- Other_____

Relational

- Grief is disruptive and disorienting
- Grief is the recognition that I have lost someone I love
- Grief can also be the recognition that I was supposed to care about the loved one who died, but I didn't. This disconnect makes me feel isolated
- There is a change in who I am now
- There is a change in how I relate to others
- There is a change in how others relate to me
- Other_____

Physical

Physical symptoms brought on by grief:

- Lack of energy
- Headaches
- Can't sleep
- Unable to concentrate
- Little appetite
- Illness brought on by stress
- Other_____

Perceptual

Grief is a sensation

- It can feel like an amputee who has lost a limb; part of myself
- The deeper my emotional involvement, the deeper my grief wound
- The more significant my loss, the more intense my grief disables me like a sickness
- Grief is an injury that needs time to heal
- It takes courage to grieve, a desire to be healthy while grieving
- It has broken my heart, it has broken me
- Other_____

Spiritual

Grief can feel hopeless

- God abandoned me
- I don't know how God's going to bring anything good out of this

- I feel further from the Lord
- God is not in control
- The Holy Spirit is not comforting me as I need
- Anger at God
- Other_____

Cultural/Societal

Grief is unique to me
- My personality
- My church culture
- My ethnicity
- My family
- My extended family
- Previous deaths
- Other_____

Circling the items above helps you visually see the different areas in your life that have been touched by grief. These areas are varied and widespread…this is grief.

FINAL THOUGHTS

YOU ARE AMAZING! This is not easy. In the following chapters, there will be hard work surrounding the grief you are experiencing. The reason you go back to the grief is not to stay in it, but to complete it.

Each chapter has exercises that may require more writing than the space provided in the workbook. Get additional sheets of paper or a journal to give you more room to write down your thoughts.

To receive the most benefit from this study, set aside time every day to sit with God and listen. In Scripture it says that

Jesus often spent time alone with His Father. If Jesus needed to do that, then you definitely need to do it, too. In addition, choose to talk with Him throughout the day. He will guide you through the Holy Spirit. He promises!

Bible Verses

At the beginning and end of each chapter are Bible verses. You may want to highlight or underline these in your Bible. The time will come when this study is over. Grief will linger. Whenever you open your Bible you will see God's words for you.

May God himself, the God of peace, sanctify you through and through. May your whole spirit, soul and body be kept blameless at the coming of our Lord Jesus Christ. The one who calls you is faithful, and he will do it. 1 Thessalonians 5:23–24

Let us approach the throne of grace with confidence, so that we may receive mercy and find grace to help us in our time of need. Hebrews 4:16

…the Spirit helps us in our weakness. We do not know what we ought to pray for, but the Spirit himself intercedes for us with groans that words cannot express. Romans 8:26

CHAPTER 2

Unique Grief
My Broken Bowl, My Broken Life

In my distress, I called to the LORD; I cried to my God for help...He reached down from on high and took hold of me: he drew me out of deep waters. Psalm 18:6,16

Chapter 1 discussed types of grief, your responses to your loss and how it can interfere with the ability to care for your daily needs. This chapter looks at the pieces of your "broken bowl," how your pieces are part of your grief, and how those pieces are unique to you. Each piece represents a way you have been changed by the death of your loved one/s.

CONTRIBUTORS TO YOUR GRIEF

Listed below are factors that can either assist you in grieving or prevent "good grief." What makes you who you are contributes to your grief journey. Take time now to jot down your thoughts about each of these categories. Ask God to show you wisdom about yourself and how you do or do not grieve.

REFLECT: To help tell my grief story, circle the ones that apply and write down any notes:

My Current Support System while I grieve: (write down names)
- Family members
- Social friends

- Work friends
- School friends
- Church friends
- I have no apparent support system
- Other_____
- Notes

My Unique Personality (before my loss):

- Experiential: passionate, excitable, temperamental, feeling
- Analytical: logical, left-brained, systematic
- Outgoing: extrovert, affectionate, easygoing
- Reserved: introvert, quiet, private
- Other_____
- Notes

Societal, Cultural, and Religious Influences affecting my grieving:

- Generation of deceased
- Family expectations around grieving
- Friends expectations about how I am to grieve
- Religious belief or no belief of deceased
- My religious preference
- Other_____
- Notes

Spiritual Influences affecting my grieving:

- Secular v. Christian perspective of those grieving
- Secular v. Christian perspective of my loved one/s
- My faith was not very active prior to the death
- My faith was active and strong prior to the death
- Other_____
- Notes

Current Crises/Stresses in my Life affecting my grieving:

- Caretaker responsibilities for an elder
- Children/grandchildren/siblings/spouse of deceased
- Daily living
- Work responsibilities
- Health concerns
- Previous ungrieved loss/es
- Other_____
- Notes

My Past Experiences with Loss:

- Geographic move
- Job/school change
- Significant financial changes
- Relationship losses
- Smooth life with little experience with loss

- Other deaths of loved ones
- Other _____
- Notes

Think back to those misconceptions that were discussed in Chapter 1. These too affect grieving and mourning. Look at the above items you circled and know that no one else has the same contributing factors or identical stories as you do. Your grief is unique and only you have experienced what you have been through.

A Note on Medication

Death of a loved one can alter the effectiveness of medication you are currently taking. Please be sure to consult your physician to assess pharmaceutical efficacy during this time.

Death of a loved one can also be a time where medication is necessary. Caution is important here. Medication to assist you in daily functioning may be advantageous. However, medication that numbs to the point of memory loss or causes the inability to feel and experience grief may only prolong the recovery process.

Consult with professionals to evaluate your situation.

LOOKING AT YOUR GRIEF

There is much research on grief and how one "deals" with it. This research has produced many models on grief. The following are two grief models for your education. Both are valid ways to interpret grief. You may connect with one of them or you may find you see yourself in both depending on different circumstances in your life. They are used here not to categorize you or make you feel like you are not "measuring up," but to help you see that your grief journey is YOUR grief journey and that only you can identify the factors that are unique to you and your loss. Use these models to help you see yourself more clearly and work towards healing in areas that are keeping you in a state of brokenness.

#1 — Stages Model by Kubler-Ross

This first model has found that "common experiences" or stages of grief can be universal and experienced by people from all walks of life and across many cultures. This model of grief was first suggested by Elisabeth Kubler-Ross in the book *On Death and Dying*. She proposed that people who are grieving can go through stages, but do not necessarily go through them in the same order or experience all of them. According to Kubler-Ross, these stages were meant to "normalize" your grief and give you comfort. (Devine, 2014)

Take a look at the following stages. Remember, these phases are fluid — you can be in more than one and shift between them as time advances.

Denial (Shock): At first, it may be difficult to accept that your loved one has died. Some cry, but others are too numb. They're in shock. Shock acts as a defense against the painful feelings associated with loss. Shock is nature's way of helping you through what otherwise seems unbearable.

Anger (Explosive emotions): Anger, bitterness, hostility and resentment are common emotions experienced by a grieving person. These feelings may come on suddenly and without explanation, or may emerge gradually. These types of feelings, while uncomfortable, are no cause for shame. It's best just to accept your emotions and express them in healthy ways. NOTE: Please refrain from emotionally assaulting someone you may feel is responsible. It may only make a tough situation worse.

Bargaining (Guilt): This is defined by feelings of guilt and anger that may occur at the same time. Some people may feel guilty because of their angry feelings. Others feel guilty about something that was said or done that is now regretted. Still others may experience guilt if they believe they could have done something to prevent the deceased person's illness or death. Such nagging thoughts often begin with "if only" or "what if." If only we had called the doctor sooner. What if we had recognized the symptoms earlier?

Depression (Loss and loneliness): As shock lessens, feelings of uncertainty, confusion or disorganization often set in and can lead to depression. All of the activities associated with everyday life may seem unimportant given the major loss you've experienced. A person's normal routine is now forever changed.

Loss and loneliness are often the most painful of emotions and involves acknowledging the significance of the loss. Many people will feel depressed and will withdraw from activities they previously enjoyed. They may feel a sense of emptiness and lack of purpose. NOTE: Lack of activity can be very appropriate for some. Yet it needs to be monitored to protect from too much debilitation.

Acceptance (Relief and recovery): Feelings of relief and a sense that the worst is over comes with the realization that life will go on and that you will be all right. It is important to realize that feeling relief in no way diminishes the loss you have experienced. It simply marks the beginning of recovery.

REFLECT: By identifying my thoughts and emotions, I am able to place the loss outside myself so I can take a look at it.

- In this model, what is beneficial for me?

- What is not helpful for me?

- What stage am I in now? How do I know this?

#2 — Dual Process Model by Stroebe and Schut

In the dual process model developed by Stroebe and Schut, grief is viewed as an active, non-linear process, where at times you face your grief and at other times you avoid it. This model discusses "loss-oriented" and "restoration-oriented" stresses related to your loss.

Loss-oriented stresses are related to the <u>actual</u> loss. Thoughts and emotions about the actual loss is an example of a loss-oriented stress. During your daily living, you either confront or avoid them. For example, when life responsibilities happen, your focus and attention is there, and you purposefully put your grief on hold to accomplish life's duties (avoid). Then life responsibilities slow down and you have time to express your grief and remember your loved one/s (confront).

Restoration-oriented stresses deal with losses and changes that <u>result</u> from the loss (these are called secondary losses later in this chapter). Examples of these stresses can be role changes in the family or having to learn new skills. Like loss-oriented stresses, restoration-oriented stresses can be confronted or avoided. For example, a woman's husband died and she needs to work. She can either wait for a job to fall in her lap (avoid) or she can start the process of looking for a job (confront).

After the death of your loved one/s, you can constantly shift back and forth between loss-orientation and restoration-orientation. There is a time for loss and a time for restoration in grief. This is normal. This model also states that there is a time to confront and a time to avoid your stresses. It is important to take a break from the task of grieving in order to take care of life duties and everyday needs. Your grief is experienced in doses similar to medicine (called dosing your grief), which can be managed throughout the day.

This model allows for variations based on personal, cultural, familial, social, and other variables of a person. It recognizes grief as a process of dealing with stresses from the actual loss and grief brought about by secondary losses. (Humphrey, 2009)

REFLECT:

- In this model, what is beneficial for me?

- What is not helpful for me?

- Recall a time when I was "dosing my grief." Write it down:

More on Models

There are many models and theories on grief. Grief models are developed to help put some "structure" on something that is complex and complicated. They are not inclusive and you will discover that your grief may not follow a set pattern.

CHAPTER 2: UNIQUE GRIEF   21

Keep in mind:

- A model is a concept and there are many of them
- Grief can be like a plate of spaghetti noodles; it goes all over the place and in a seemingly haphazard fashion
- A "stage" is not what you get through before you progress to the next, and you may experience a "stage" more than once
- A model is not complete and does not address every issue and feeling that is experienced in grief
- Remnants of grief will always be with you

Remember that your grief experience is unique to you. Whatever ways you experience grief, all your thoughts and feelings can seem all mixed up, going from one emotion to the next. Your grief process can look more like the following:

Figure 2.1

STAGES OF GRIEF	My experience

Loss-Hurt	Loss Adjustment	Loss-Hurt	Loss Adjustment
Shock	Helping Others	Shock	Helping Others
Numbness	Affirmation	Numbness	Affirmation
Denial	Hope	Denial	Hope
Emotional Outbursts	New Patterns	Emotional Outbursts	New Patterns
Anger	New Strengths	Anger	New Strengths
Fear		Fear	
Searchings	New Relationships	Searchings	New Relationships
Disorganization	"Re-Entry" Troubles	Disorganization	"Re-Entry" Troubles
Panic	Depression	Panic	Depression
Loneliness		Loneliness	
Guilt	Isolation	Guilt	Isolation

Source: public domain

SECONDARY LOSSES

Death will undoubtedly lead to secondary losses that occur as a direct result of your primary loss. Some of these secondary losses are noticed immediately and some reveal themselves over time. Often, those grieving feel like they have not only lost the person, they have lost *everything*. These secondary losses are important to be recognized as an integral part of your complex and unique grief journey.

REFLECT: Circle any of the following that I have or am experiencing:

Loss of Relationship

- Lost my confidant, source of laughter, lover
- Lost a relationship as a result of end-of-life squabbles
- Lost my walking partner, movie companion, sense of safety
- Lost my cook, mechanic, gardener, driver, technology guru
- Loss of digital/social media connection
- I am blamed by others for the loved one's death
- Other_____

Loss of Material Things

- Loss of Financial Security
- Loss of Home
- Loss of Lifestyle
- Other_____

Loss of Role in the Home

- Tasks I once did I no longer need to do
- Tasks I never had to do are now my responsibility
- Other_____

Loss of Role in the Family

- Loss of caregiver role or assuming caregiver role due to loss
- My designation as child, spouse, parent, grandparent changed
- Family has distanced themselves from me,
  - especially_____
- Other_____

Loss of Role at Work

- My ability to work is affected
- My performance is affected
- My relationships at work are affected
- Other_____

Loss of Role among Friends

- I feel out of place in my social settings
- I lost my "mom group," or "couple's group" friends, sports buddies
- Friends distanced themselves
- Other_____

Loss of Role in the Community

- I feel uncomfortable going to my usual meeting spots
- I was an active volunteer and now feel unmotivated
- Other_____

Loss of Hopes, Dreams, Expectations

- I had an expectation of what my future looked like
- Events that I used to look forward to will no longer take place

- I believed my loved one would get well
- Hopes of reconciliation with the person who died can no longer be resolved
- Other_____
- Any additional thoughts/emotions related to these secondary losses

Grief is a unique and individual process. Listen to your own experiences. While this is hard, you are doing great.

EXERCISE: JOURNAL MY GRIEF STORY

Having taken a look at the circumstances surrounding the loss of my loved one/s, it's time to start recording my unique story.

REMEMBER: There is no right or wrong way to do this. Just start writing whatever comes to mind. Remember my "bowl" has been broken. The following prompts will help put some order to the various web of facts, emotions, and impact I am experiencing.

MEDITATE: This is my story:

- When did the death occur?

- How did I learn about my loved one/s death?

- What was my relationship like with my loved one at the time of their death?

- What were the circumstances around the death?

- Who was supporting or not supporting me at this time?

- Was there a funeral service or life celebration? If yes, what happened?

- Other important facts to share

WRITE: It is time to put my story on paper. By placing it "outside of me", this gives me a tiny space in which to breathe. My broken bowl can be viewed, walked around, and touched. The racing in my mind slows as I have a place to put the pieces. Get a journal or sheets of paper to write as needed. Write much or a little. Set it aside and return to it later. Add to it or change it. It is my story to tell and mine alone.

ACTION: Share my grief story in group or with a caring friend.

FINAL THOUGHTS

PRAY: O Father, You are the God who sees me! You are the One that knows all the cracks and stress fractures that no one else can see. Help me to understand that all of the pieces of my life which make me unique are the same pieces that make my grief and brokenness different from others. Help me see the person You see in me so that I can begin to put the pieces back together. I ask these things in Your holy name. Amen.

Death is not God's original plan. He designed you to be in relationship with Him for eternity. Then the Fall occurred, and with it came death on many levels. Yet God in Jesus created and led the way for each of us to be back in perfect relationship with Him eternally. God will create new life for you out of the broken bowl, which rests in front of you now.

It is amazing to "see" the ways that death can bring even the smallest cracks to your bowl. What looked shattered is now more fragmented. Yet we have a good God who WILL bring you through this.

Bible Verses

Be merciful to me, O Lord, for I am in distress; my eyes grow weak with sorrow, my soul and body with grief. Psalm 31:9

Blessed are those who mourn, for they will be comforted... Matthew 5:4

When you pass through the waters, I will be with you; and when you pass through the rivers, they will not sweep over you. When you walk through the fire, you will not be burned; the flames will not set you ablaze. Isaiah 43:2

So do not fear, for I am with you; do not be dismayed, for I am your God. Isaiah 41:10

CHAPTER 3

Emotions
My Shattered Bowl

Jesus wept. John 11:35

Chapter 2 discussed how your journey is unique and you learned that your grief, your life, and your circumstances are influential in your grieving process. This chapter will take a look at how your emotional "broken pieces" can affect your grief.

EMOTIONS

The feelings associated with the loss of a loved one can be intense, confusing and sometimes conflicting. They can change abruptly and unpredictably and will likely not occur in a particular order. You cannot check them off a list as if finished and then move on to another. You may be sobbing or upset one moment and then have joy for what God is doing in your life the next moment. Refer back to Figure 2.1 to review your experience of grief.

Some of the feelings you may be experiencing are listed below. They are grouped based on similar emotion, but are not exclusive to that grouping. You will likely experience some of them, but not all of them. Identifying them can help you heal and realize that they are normal in grief. Remember, there are no wrong emotions.

REFLECT: Below is a list of emotions I have or will experience through the grief. Many of the items are taken from the book *Understanding Your Grief* by Wolfelt (2003). Circle the ones that I identify with:

- **Initial Feeling** - Self-protection
  - Shock, Numbness, Denial, Disbelief
- **Explosive Emotion** - Protest
  - Anger, Blame, Terror, Resentment, Rage, Jealousy
- **Searching** - Fragmented
  - Disorganized, Confused, Helplessness, Emptiness, Yearning
- **Feeling Insecure** - Unsafe, Unsure
  - Anxiety, Fear, Panic, Overwhelmed, Pre-occupation, Helplessness, Vulnerable
- **Guilt and Regret** - If only
  - Blame, Bitterness, Betrayal, Abandonment, Distrust
- **Sadness/Depression** - It hurts
  - Loneliness, Detachment, Feeling Lost, Despair, Anguish, Sorrow, Hopelessness
- **Relief and Release** - Re-entry
  - Hope, Whole, Strengthened, Gratefulness, New patterns, Affirmation
- Other_____

Choose one dominant feeling from the preceding list.

WRITE: Are there any insights into why that feeling is so powerful? Ask God for knowledge about why this is such a strong emotion.

Though you have made me see troubles, many and bitter, you will restore my life again; from the depths of the earth you will again bring me up. Psalm 71:20

There aren't any "shoulds" with respect to how grief is felt or expressed. It's common for people who have lost someone close to feel sad, angry, helpless, guilty, anxious, lonely and frightened. It is also common to experience a sense of shock or numbness, especially if the death was sudden and unexpected. All of these feelings are normal, though not pleasant, and they can all be part of the process of grief. The key is to accept your feelings, whatever they may be, and not deny them or push them away. This may be very difficult, since it can be quite painful to allow yourself to experience the many emotions of grief.

What if you're not feeling "normal and acceptable" grief?

You had a challenging relationship with the person who died. The relationship was difficult to a level of dislike. Maybe they were hurtful to you and those you loved. Maybe they were violent and abusive. Maybe they were toxic or betrayed you. Maybe their dysfunction created the need to distance yourself emotionally and physically. Regardless of the cause, you may feel numb or conflicted about the death of this "loved" one. That's your story of grief.

DO continue going through the GOLD workbook. Do not let the lack of emotion or negative feelings towards the deceased deter you from healing.

BALL OF GRIEF

Think of the circumstances and relationship with your loved one/s. Review Chapter 2 where you listed some of the circumstances that make your grief journey unique.

The following diagram is the "Ball of Grief." It gives a visual interpretation of what your various and diverse emotions may be surrounding your loss.

Write: Look at the emotions. Notice how the emotions are intertwined with each other, how some of them appear more than once. Grab some markers or colored pencils and color in the emotions you experience as a result of the death. Use one or as many different colors as you would like.

You may have the entire ball filled or a few key sections. This is for your personal benefit to help you determine which emotions you struggle with.

FIGURE 3.1

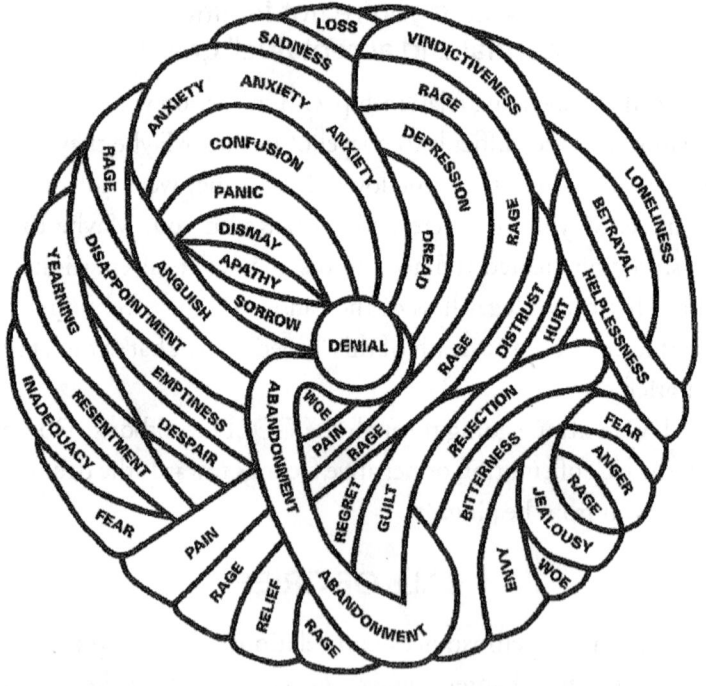

Ball of Grief • A Tangled "Ball" of Emotions

Source: Wright, n.d.

REFLECT: Looking at the ball of emotions, what are three that affect me the most? Write them here:

1.
2.
3.

PRAY: God, show me how You are with me in these emotions. Amen

WHAT GRIEVES GOD

In God's sovereignty, He allows grief and suffering. Even Jesus was a suffering Savior…but he did not stay there. Look at the following Bible verses and write down your responses:

How does Jesus model His response to grief in *John 11:33*:

Grieving is actually a show of faith. You are trusting Jesus to hold you at your most vulnerable time.

- What does it say in *Job 36:15*:

- *Proverbs 3: 5–6:*

- *Psalm 42:2–7:*

- *Psalm 142:1–3:*

PRAY: Father, You are always with me. You are always with me… even when I don't want to be with You. You want to hear my voice and heart no matter what is in it. Help me to be quiet amidst the chaos of life so I can just be with You, hear You, and experience Your peace in the depths of my heart. Amen

I have a Savior whose life was shattered for me.

WHAT TO DO WITH ALL THESE EMOTIONS

- **Accept Them:** Emotions are given to us by God. They are part of being human.
- **Think and Feel Them:** Allow yourself to think and feel. The more we try to deny, hide, or "keep them under control," the more they take hold. The way to deal with feelings is to experience them and release them in a variety of ways.
- **Cry:** Tears act to relieve your heart. Let them flow and know they are natural and cleansing, even though it may be uncomfortable to cry.
- **Get Moving:** Physical activity can help to ease your pain. It can help reduce stress and other built up thoughts and emotions.
- **Learn About Them:** Engaging your head with your heart helps make you whole. If identifying your feelings is unfamiliar for you, ask someone to help you.
- **Talk About Them:**

- Choose someone you can trust to listen and receive your story over and over again. Choose a person who will hold you safely and won't let you go it alone.
- Talk to your loved one. This helps keep their memory alive and may comfort you. This is different than talking to the dead. This is simply directing the expression of your thoughts and emotions to your loved one.
- **Write About Them:**
  - Write in a journal to capture your thoughts and feelings. You may be able to express and see your emotions in a new way.
  - Write a letter to your loved one who died. Getting your feelings out on paper helps you "see them" and release them.
  - Write your prayers to God. He is always with you and wants to hear your heart. Listen to His still, soft voice within you. Seek it. Follow it.
- **Turn to God — Over and Over Again:** Though our thoughts, feelings, and circumstances change, God does not change. He promises to be with us always. *I the Lord do not change. Malachi 3:6*
- **Befriend Your Emotions:** Do not be discouraged. Know that God will surely fulfill all of your needs. Keep remembering that. It will help you not expect this fulfillment from people who you already know, that are incapable of giving it. (Nouwen, 1996)
- **Ask God to Give You Patience and Understanding for Yourself:** When your life has been shattered and your heart broken, God can pick up the pieces, hold you and begin to put you back together. Accept compassion for yourself, just as you would want others to receive it from you.

- **Seek Professional Help as Needed:**
  - If your grief is so overwhelming and continues to interfere with your everyday functioning at home, work or life in general, you may need additional help.
  - Seeking help is healthy.

EXERCISE: GRIEF LETTER OF EMOTIONS

All these emotions are overwhelming, aren't they? It's time to express those emotions to someone. It's time to write a letter directed to the loved one who died, some other person, or even God. This letter is not intended to be mailed. It doesn't have to be "nice or polite."

REMEMBER: Write the thoughts and emotions from my heart. Express my true self and where I am NOW. If I am writing to God, remember that he wants me to run to Him, to cry out to Him, to bring ALL of what I need.

MEDITATE: To help me figure out who to write to, think about the following: Who am I mad at? Who hurt me? Who left me?

The following is an example of one person's letter:

Figure 3.2: Sample Letter

> Dear God,
>
> I write this letter to you to get my feelings out about the death of my mother-in-law, Linda. She died a painful death from cancer but it was quick and for that I am grateful. My major feelings of struggle are toward family. I am resentful that my two sisters-in-law took no responsibility to help in her care or service for her. I resent their unfairness and lack of empathy. I realize I want life to be fair. I hoped for all of Linda's family to show care and love for one another.
>
> Secondly, I initially felt anxious when we realized how she needed hospice care and was dying — what am I to do? I have learned that I react to change or perceived lack of control with anxiety. This caused my blood pressure to rise dangerously high. Help me understand my own needs to take care of myself and what my part is in being a loving daughter-in-law and wife.
>
> Third, I feel relief for Linda. Her pain is over and she left this earth as she wanted — she had been showing signs of illness for the past year but would not receive medical help. It was her determination to die without lots of treatment, cost or attention. Only in the last month of her life did she concede how much she was in pain and became very weak. She died on Christmas Day in the loving arms of Jesus.
>
> Lord, I need Your loving arms to wrap around me, to calm me and to remove my anger and resentment so that I may have serenity. Remove my need for fairness on this earth even though I know that You are in control. Help me to lay all of this at Your feet and listen to only the Holy Spirit to guide and comfort me.

Remember, this letter is not meant to be mailed. This is for me to put my thoughts outside myself and place them before God.

WRITE: This letter is to express what I need. Start writing now. Share this in my group or with a caring friend.

FINAL THOUGHTS

After you pass the initial shock and disbelief that your loved one has really died, your heart will begin to feel again — and with this reality comes pain. Your heart has been wounded and it hurts — your emotions are like a mirror showing what is in your heart. You may feel that you cannot survive — or even want to survive — without your loved one. The pain will come and go and gradually lessen as you work your way through your grief.

In the book *A Grief Disguised*, author Jerry Sittser (2004) wrote that "the quickest way to reach the light of day is not to chase the sunset, but rather to head through the darkness to the sunrise." Avoiding the grieving and mourning process is to chase the sunset.

Thank you for having the courage to do this workbook and be willing to head through the darkness. As you collect the pieces of your broken bowl, lift them up as if to fit them together again. See the Light through the cracks. Jesus is in the cracks. He will make a new creation, different than before.

Bible Verses

He was despised and rejected by mankind, a man of suffering and familiar with pain. Like one from whom people hide their faces he was despised, and we held him in low esteem. Isaiah 53:3

The Lord is close to the brokenhearted and saves those who are crushed in spirit. Psalm 34:18

CHAPTER 4

Why
Why Did My Bowl Break

I say to God my Rock, "Why have you forgotten me?
Why must I go about mourning, oppressed by the enemy?"
My bones suffer mortal agony as my foes taunt me, saying to
me all day long, "Where is your God?" Psalm 42:9–10

Chapter 3 discussed emotions you may have surrounding the grief you are experiencing. Acknowledging them takes the broken pieces out of hiding and brings them to the light where they can begin to mend. This chapter will continue to explore emotions and thoughts, spending time asking questions surrounding your loss.

QUESTIONS

"It's not fair that my sister was killed by a drunk driver. She was so young." "My husband was getting ready to retire. Why did he have to suffer and die from cancer?" "Why don't I feel sad about this person dying?" "Why did God allow my loved one to die? Why would a loving God do such a thing?"

Through the ages, human beings have sought to reconcile their own understanding and circumstances with the seemingly endless suffering around them. When tragedy strikes, we want to know WHY?

What are your WHY questions? For example: Why did that have to happen? Why did they have to die? Why wasn't I there to prevent the accident? Why did they have to suffer?

REFLECT: God knows me better than I know myself, so no holding back what is inside of me. Write down all my WHY questions here.

PRAY: God continue to show me any questions I have, any deep place I need to put before You. Thank you that You are God and You know what I need to say. Amen

WHY AM I ANGRY?

Anger. It's a natural emotion that everyone experiences. Sometimes it is appropriate and desired, and sometimes it is illogical and unwanted. Anger is beneficial when expressed in healthy ways with constructive boundaries. It becomes unhealthy when you let it go unchecked and control you in ways damaging to yourself and others.

The most common way we see anger expressed is through outbursts, yelling, and physical expressions like hitting, throwing, and punching things. This external anger is basically easy to see. Where anger becomes more difficult to acknowledge is when it is expressed in other ways such as "annoyance, irritability, frustration, fretting, boisterous rages or withdrawing into critical thoughts or self-pity to sadness" (Carter and Minirth, 2012).

Anger says, "Why me?" "I am just plain mad at everything and everybody." "I'm mad at God." "I'm mad at the doctor." "I'm mad at my loved one for leaving me." "I'm mad at myself for not doing more."

Emotions Under Anger

Take a good hard look at your anger and questions. Oftentimes, anger is not the primary emotion. There can be other emotions underneath anger. Anger can fall into some common themes, and these themes can be at the root of your anger. <u>Loss-related</u> anger themes such as resentment/envy, pride, guilt, sadness/despair, fear/anxiety, and addiction are listed below. Circle the ones that you can relate with and write any additional thoughts under the Reflect questions:

Resentment/Envy
- Envy says, "Why did this happen to <u>me</u>? Why didn't my loved one experience the same healing that others do?" "Why did their kids get to graduate, get married…and mine didn't?" "I don't fit in anymore."
- I have resentful thoughts but I don't say them to anyone. Now my emotions are bottled up, ready to explode or implode
- I wish my loved one was living to experience what others are, but there is no one to say these thoughts to or a place to put these emotions
- I have experienced so many secondary losses that I have become resentful of what others have that I no longer do
- Other_____

Envy can lead to resentment which can quickly turn to anger.

REFLECT: What else is "envy" saying to me?

A heart at peace gives life to the body, but envy rots the bones.
Proverbs 14:30

Pride
- Pride says, "No one understands what I am going through, so I'm going to 'go it alone.' I don't need anyone's help anyway."
- I am building a wall around my heart so I only have to depend on me
- I think a lot about myself and how things affect me
- Pride disguises itself as self-sufficiency looking like I have it all together. I think I am the only one who cares about me so I might as well do it alone and not reach out to others
- Other_____

Pride can lead me to internalize my pain which can turn to anger at myself and others.

REFLECT: What else is "pride" saying to me?

You have been deceived by your own pride because you live in a rock fortress and make your home high in the mountains.
Obadiah 3:3 (NLT)

Guilt
- Guilt says, "Why didn't I recognize that something was wrong? Why didn't I see what was happening?" "Why was that the last thing I said?"
- I feel self-condemnation because of something I did
- I feel self-condemnation because of something I did not do
- Other_____

Guilt leads to anger directed squarely at myself.

REFLECT: What else is "guilt" saying to me?

My guilt has overwhelmed me like a burden too heavy to bear.
Psalm 38:4

Sadness/Despair
- Despair says, "Why won't I ever be happy again? I don't want to be happy again." "I can't have a future without my loved one."
- For me to be happy in my future, I am to forget my loved one
- I believe that my life now is filled with nothing but misery
- I have a total loss of hope
- I don't want to continue to live my changed life without my loved one
- Other_____

Despair leads to bitterness which is quickly followed by anger.

REFLECT: What else is "despair" saying to me?

The thief comes only to steal and kill and destroy…John 10:10a

Fear/Anxiety
- Anxiety says, "What am I supposed to do now? How will I pay the bills? How can I keep up with all the work this place requires? How am I supposed to be both parents to the kids?"
- My mind is spinning in circles because of a ton of unanswered thoughts and questions about my future
- I keep wondering how I am going to be able to continue on with my life without my loved one to help me
- Worrying about tomorrow wipes out all my strength for today
- Other_____

Fear and anxiety can turn inward as frustration and anger when a person feels ill-equipped to handle their new role.

REFLECT: What else is "anxiety" saying to me?

> *Therefore do not worry about tomorrow, for tomorrow will worry about itself. Each day has enough trouble of its own.*
> *Matthew 6:34*

Addiction
- Addiction says, "Have another glass of wine. It'll take the edge off." "I know you quit smoking, but you deserve it. Have one." "Eating makes me feel good, so I'm going to eat the whole bag." "Just keep working late so I don't have to think about it."
- Losing my loved one hurt so much. Now I don't want to feel anything else because feeling doesn't feel good

- I want to be numb about anything and everything so I won't feel or think
- I think that just a little bit more is ok. Then one day I woke up dependent on the drug of my choice
- Other_____

Addiction attempts to mask my pain and anger, but it is still there.

REFLECT: What else is "addiction" saying to me?

Temptation comes from our own desires, which entice us and drag us away. These desires give birth to sinful actions. And when sin is allowed to grow, it gives birth to death. James 1:14–15 (NLT)

REFLECT: Are there other ways I am expressing anger that weren't listed?

WHAT DOES THE BIBLE SAY?
JOB'S WHY QUESTIONS

Remember Job? You can learn a lot about yourself and God's character as you look to the book of Job. Job felt robbed of every sign of God's favor. He asked God many questions about suffering and death.

REFLECT: Look at some of Job's WHY questions in *Job 3* and *7* and write them down:

Job and his friends were asking many of the same questions that you ask. If God loves me, why did He let this happen? Why didn't God miraculously heal my loved one? Why didn't He answer my prayers?

You are one of thousands who throughout history ask for understanding from God.

Why Does Pain and Suffering Exist?

The original creation was a beautiful place, full of life and joy in the presence of the Creator. God created Adam and Eve and placed them in a perfect paradise.

Then evil entered and God's paradise was changed. Adam and Eve let the serpent be louder and more influential than God's voice. And from that death, pain, and suffering entered the world.

Write what these Bible verses say:

- *Genesis 2:16–17:*

- *Genesis 3:1–24:*

- *Romans 5:12:*

God's word is NOT saying that the death of your loved one is the result of him or her being punished for a specific sin. All people are human and as humans, we all face death.

Why is Job Angry?

Let's take a look at Job again and how he expressed his feelings towards God:

- What does Job think about God in *Job 9:1-11*?

- What are Job's feelings if he did reach out to God in chapter *9:16–17*?

- How does Job express his pain and anger towards God in *Job 10*? See if you can list at least ten:

- Are any of Job's responses to anger similar to yours? If yes, write them down:

For some people holding onto anger is a way to hold onto their loved one/s. Some people fight for justice, others fight to remember their loved one/s and sometimes they fight so long they forget what they are fighting for. Giving up the fight does not mean that you are giving up on your loved one. There is a way to let go of anger and hurt and keep the best parts of your loved one/s close to your heart.

Many people believe that an all-knowing merciful God would not have taken their loved one/s. Then why did their loved one die? We live in a world of brokenness where bad things happen to good people just like bad things happen to bad people. God does not cause these bad things to happen. He grieves with you. And through the grief He can and will bring good out of your loss when you allow Him to work through you.

ASKING QUESTIONS OTHER THAN WHY

When you continue to seek answers to question after question, it can turn into a game of Whac-a-Mole, the game found at pizza places and arcades. Moles pop up out of holes at random and varying frequency, then your job is to hit them with a mallet before they go back down. It's a fast paced and intense game of keeping your focus on the moles.

Your questions are also like the way war on terror has been fought in the past. The enemy's terror cells seem to randomly pop up at different locations and at times without any forewarning. The response was to fight each one as they popped up. The problem was that there was no resolution, just an endless game of chasing every terror cell.

Asking question after question regarding your loves one's death can be like the above illustrations. As soon as you answer one question regarding your loved one's death, another pops up, then another and another. Whac-a-Mole and the enemy's terror cells are like Satan's strategic game. He wants you to play along thinking you can figure it out on your own. This keeps you stuck in grief so you will continue to play in his game.

When Aaron Fechter, the inventor of Whac-a-Mole, was asked what the best strategy to playing the game was, he replied, "The technique I found most useful is to take a hit and return to the middle position above the playing field, never looking at any of the moles, but using your field of vision and peripheral vision to watch the playing field.... Just look at the whole field, and react when you see something out the corner of your eye, then immediately return to center position ready to hit the next one." (Peritz, 2015). Your part is not to look at the moles, which are your questions, but to look at the bigger picture. That bigger picture is where you let God look at your "whole field." He wants you to return to the center and to ask Him questions other than why. He wants you to trust Him in the midst of all of your questions. Besides, what would actually be different if you did know the answers to your why questions?

EXERCISE: CHANGING YOUR QUESTION

Choose one of your WHY questions from the beginning of this chapter and write it here:

REFLECT: There is pain and hurt associated with this question. Take another look at this question and ask God to reveal something good experienced during this time. Scripture says, *"And we know that in all things God works for the good of those who love him…"* Romans 8:28. Look for a positive that has come through the loss.

WRITE: Write that down here:

Pray: God, help me wait quietly as You talk to my heart and comfort me in the pain. Help me to surrender more of myself to You and tell You that I trust in Your ability to heal. Amen

WRITE: When my question is WHY, it doesn't take me anywhere except down. I end up frantically giving all my attention to the

WHY and not getting it answered anyway. When I change it to a HOW question, it can now take me upward towards God. Now I want to ask God a different question…HOW.

My HOW question is:

Look at the book of Job again. Can you see God pulling Job closer to Him through his conversation with Him?

- How does God respond to Job's distress in *Job 38:1?* *38:4–39?*

- How does Job respond to God in *42:2–6?*

God explained to Job that the world is a mystery. He wanted Job to respect that mystery and accept that the mystery is bigger than Job or his friends.

- What does it say about God *in Psalm 62:8?*

WHAT ABOUT HEAVEN?

(Segments of the following are taken from the book *What Grieving People Wish You Knew*, Guthrie 2016).

In an attempt to comfort people through their grief, many turn the conversation towards the loved one being in heaven, or at least a "better place." While this brings many a measure of comfort, in others it can induce anxiety rather than peace. Culture wants to put the Band-Aid of heaven on the hurt of losing someone we love. But what if you are not sure if your loved one is in heaven?

- Heaven is a place for those who were too young or lacked the mental capacity to make that choice for themselves. *But Jesus said, Let the little children come to me and do not hinder them, for to such belongs the kingdom of heaven. Matthew 19:14*
- None of us can ever know the full reality of another person's life or the state of another person's soul. No matter what we see on the outside or believe of another, the heart can possess private words reserved purely for Christ to see. Just because we don't see it does not mean it isn't there. God alone knows the names of those who belong to Him. *He determines the number of stars and calls them each by name. Psalms 147:4*
- God is merciful and longs to save us. *Titus 3:5* says, *He saved us, not because of righteous things we had done, but because of his mercy.* We must find rest in our merciful God who loves to save, not in a person's evidence of having been saved.
- None of us is good enough for heaven. Heaven is a place for any of us who have made the deliberate decision to put their confidence in Christ's righteousness, not their own. Even the thief on the cross in his final moment called upon Jesus to save him. While we are called to produce fruit of our faith, it is faith that saves us, not the fruit. *Jesus, remember me when You come in Your kingdom! And He said to him, Truly I say to you, today you shall be with Me in Paradise. Luke 23: 42–43*

Even if you have the assurance that your loved one is in heaven, it is still perfectly normal to grieve the earthly loss. If you have received Jesus as your Lord and Savior, He can give you a peace that transcends understanding.

What if you haven't accepted Jesus that way? What's holding you back? It's time to make a decision. You have a choice - to accept all God says and bring Jesus into your life or say "No, I don't want you Jesus."

Do you want to consider getting to know God — the Creator, Provider, and Healer? This mighty, amazing, and loving God who is wild and unchanging? Ask Jesus to help you. Simply say, "Jesus, show me what to do. Even though I don't know you very well, I do know that I haven't done too well on my own. Trying to meet my own needs has not worked. Please join me, forgive me, save me. You know my heart."

Now go tell someone that you have asked Jesus to be your Savior. You will never be the same.

And heaven still feels very far away for those of us still on earth. We can know that we will be with Jesus and that is the truth that is most important to hold on to.

- What does *John 8:32* tell us about truth:

FINAL THOUGHTS

Holding onto anger is not a way to hold onto the person you lost. You may feel that giving up the anger and fight may mean that you are giving up on your loved one/s. But this is not so.

There is a way to let go of the anger and hurt while at the same time keeping the best parts of your loved one safely tucked inside your heart.

God invites you to come to Him for comfort. He weeps with you! He wants you to trust in who He is. To focus on what you know is true about Him. He wants you to trust Him even in the midst of all your pain and anguish.

PRAY: Dear Jesus, I am grieving, and I need your help. I know that I am a sinner and that my actions against God has separated me from You. But I believe that You experienced the punishment that should have been mine by dying on the cross for my sins. I believe You rose from the dead so I could have the hope of living forever with You instead of spending eternity separated from You. Thank you for enduring the grief and the pain to show Your love for me. I place my trust in You to help me heal. Amen.

Bible Verses

God saw all that he had made, and it was very good. Genesis 1:31

For God so loved the world that he gave his one and only Son, that whoever believes in him shall not perish but have eternal life. John 3:16

He looked around at them in anger and, deeply distressed at their stubborn hearts, said to the man, "Stretch out your hand." He stretched it out, and his hand was completely restored. Mark 3:5

CHAPTER 5
Life Losses
Broken Pieces in My Bowl

Blessed are those who mourn for they shall be comforted. Matthew 5:4

Chapter 4 focused on questions, identifying the true emotions behind anger, and looking at how your grief may be similar to Job's questions and anger. This chapter looks at contributors to your grief including complicated relationships and secondary losses.

WHY IT'S COMPLICATED

For some people, feelings of loss are debilitating and don't improve even after time passes. This is known as *complicated grief*, which was briefly discussed in Chapter 1. In complicated grief, painful emotions are so long lasting and severe that you have trouble accepting the loss and resuming your own life. You may tend to isolate yourself from others, because you believe there is no way they can possibly understand your pain. You feel as though you cannot find a new identity without your loved one. Or maybe you are bitter, angry or resentful towards God or others. Or you feel guilt, shame or even responsibility for the death. You are angry at your loved one/s for leaving you. You are stuck and unable to move forward in any sort of healthy or positive way.

When stuck in grief, an honest assessment is important to help identify the areas where healing needs to take place.

Complicated Relationships

For better or worse, being stuck in grief can say more about the relationship than it does about the grieving process. With this relationship loss, life seems incomplete and different than what you imagined it was going to be. Things were left undone; things were left unsaid. For instance, what if you didn't like certain aspects of the person who died (they were controlling, they had a mean temperament, they didn't talk to you, they didn't love you in ways that you wanted…)? Or you could have lost a relationship that was so important to you that you're left holding emptiness. Your thoughts and emotions surrounding that person can complicate your grief process.

REFLECT:

- What if years ago my relationship was good, but it never grew once the kids were gone. I found out we didn't have anything in common anymore or that we even liked each other
- The person who died was abusive to me
- The person was ill and I have a sense of relief even though others may expect me not to feel this way
- I am missing the hopes and dreams of what "could have been"; the life I was wanting to live
- Others

How to deal with it? It's OK to think as you do. Grieve the lost dreams. Appreciate the relief. Don't let others dictate what you "must" experience about the death. The more complicated the relationship, the more complicated your grief.

Secondary Losses

Life contains a variety of losses. Big ones, small ones, forgotten ones, memorable ones, painful ones, necessary ones…Looking back at these secondary losses and major events helps you see what influences your current grieving. Looking back is not to dwell on the past but to inform and propel you towards healing. How did you handle or not handle these past losses? How do they impact your current loss?

A life filled with many deep accumulated losses shapes a person's current loss of a loved one. A life with little experience of loss shapes a person's current loss, also. Neither one is harder or more painful than the other. Just different.

REFLECT: God is close to the broken-hearted. What else does scripture say?

- *Psalm 10: 17*

- *Hebrews 12: 11*

PRAY: Father God, thank you for never giving up on me. You know the hurt places in my life. Reveal the losses and help me uncover those painful places. You do this not to harm me, but as an act of loving me. Let me experience your love right now. In Jesus' name, Amen.

EXERCISE: LIFE TIMELINE

A life timeline helps identify the losses and events in my life that may be contributing to my current grief. I do this to help recognize how I have lived with and through those losses.

Look at the sample timeline in Figure 5.1 below.

FIGURE 5.1

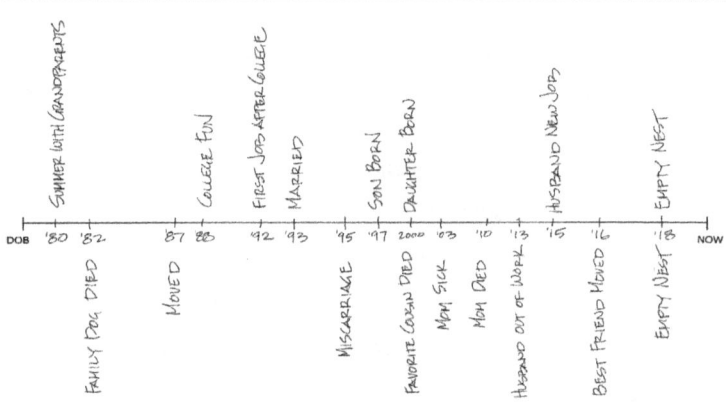

REMEMBER: I have looked at losses related to the death of my loved one/s. Now I want to take a look at secondary losses. (Look back at secondary losses and emotions previously identified in Chapter 2 to help start to put the pieces together.)

MEDITATE: Think about any additional losses that accompany major life events or past hurts. Some examples of these may include:

Birth of siblings	Change of school
Miscarriage	Death of person/pet
Lost friendships	Divorce (yours /parents)
Abuse	Relationship breakup
Job loss	Unrealized goals/dreams
Infertility	Compromised safety

Chapter 5: Life Losses

Abortion   False accusations
Empty nest   Illness/Injury
Relocation   Financial loss
Retirement   Rejection
Failure

- Other

WRITE: Now it's time to plot my life timeline.

- The line represents my life. Put my date of birth (DOB) on the far-left side of the line and today's date at the far-right side.
- Chart out my major life events on the line. Put loss events below the line and happy events above the line. Date each event.

FIGURE 5.2: My Timeline Here

Chapter 5: Life Losses

MEDITATE: Looking over my timeline losses, put an * by the one that hurt me the most. Write it down here:

WRITE: With this identified loss, answer the following questions:
- What caused this to hurt so much?

- Did I grieve this event or did I just go on with my life?

- Circle the word below to gauge how I am grieving or have grieved this event:

  Never   Barely   Sometimes   Frequently   In a good place now

- Do I have a sense that maybe that event is not finished? Why or why not?

REMEMBER: Identify 2-3 other significant losses from my timeline. Write them down here:

WRITE: God, reveal to me any theme/s surrounding these significant losses (i.e. abandonment, bitterness, codependency. There can be all kinds of loss themes). Write the theme/s down:

You are brave. Recalling and writing down your past losses was hard and brought up painful memories. This brings the dark into God's illuminating light. Placing all the losses and related emotions outside of yourself refocuses your heart for God's interaction, love, and healing.

FINAL THOUGHTS

Your life is filled with happy events and losses giving you a more complete picture of you. Yours is a life filled with a variety of experiences that has shaped you into the person you are now. Taking a "deeper dive" into the contributors to your grief is a way to look honestly and more thoroughly at your life losses.

Identifying your life losses requires intimately looking at your life - digging into your past, uncovering life events, looking at patterns, and doing the hard work. God uses it all.

God is and was in the places of loss in your past. He is in your current loss. He will be with you in the future. His love and light continually shine.

Bible Verses

What, then, shall we say in response to these things? If God is for us, who can be against us? Romans 8:31

The memory of the righteous is a blessing. Proverbs 10:7 (RSV)

Peace I leave with you; my peace I give you. I do not give to you as the world gives. Do not let your hearts be troubled and do not be afraid. John 14:27

CHAPTER 6

Stuck In Grief
My Pieces Can't Go Back the Same Way

For though we live in the world, we do not wage war as the world does. The weapons we fight with are not the weapons of the world. On the contrary, they have divine power to demolish strongholds. 2 Corinthians 10:3–4

In the previous chapter, you examined life losses and how they impact you now. This chapter will take a deeper dive into ways people may be stuck through strongholds.

STRONGHOLDS

What is a stronghold?

- According to Merriam Webster a stronghold (n.d.) is a "fortified place or a place of security or survival, a place that has been fortified so as to protect it against attack." Think of a fortress with high walls surrounding it.

- Mental health professionals recognize strongholds as something that begins as a coping mechanism during a difficult season of life, but unintentionally grows to a more significant attachment. It becomes such a familiar part of your life that you don't even realize it as a stronghold. No one ever sets out to have a stronghold.

- In a spiritual sense, Beth Moore (2009) defines a stronghold as "anything that exalts itself in our minds, 'pretending' to be bigger and more powerful than our God." Whatever the stronghold, it is something that consumes so much of your emotional and mental energy that it is impossible to live the life God desires for you.

Strongholds are built by putting up walls and barricades that you think will protect you, but they only serve to shut out the good things that remain in your life. Just as a military stronghold was typically built on high ground to have the best vantage point to see enemies approaching, our self-erected "walls" are also built on high ground. Soon that high ground begins to appear higher than God Himself. When you put your trust in something other than God, even momentarily, that allows Satan the opening he needs to gain a foothold in you and deepen his deception. His best strategy is to keep you rooted in a past life of sin, sorrow, and fear so you cannot view your current loss with any other perspective.

Some Strongholds That Keep You Stuck

In week 4, you looked at anger themes surrounding your questions and possible sources of your anger. <u>The reality is this: if you are stuck in your grief, one or more of these themes has likely become a stronghold.</u>

The following list are strongholds that have the same names as the themes from the previous chapter. Now is the time to take a closer look at these strongholds and identify how they are destructive to you. You will see how they have infiltrated your life, keeping you from living fully. They can also keep you from grieving well.

Anger

Chapter 4 contains a good deal of information about anger. Additionally, anger is often a misunderstood and/or misidentified emotion. We typically think of anger as outbursts, but anger can show up as withdrawal, crying or even physical ailments such as headaches or stomachaches. An outward explosion of anger is a chaotic event which can lead to the destruction of other people and relationships. An implosion of anger is an inward collapse, which may or may not affect other people or things, but it does lead to the destruction of oneself as was seen in the anger themes in the previous chapter. Anger itself is a normal emotion; it is what one does with it that can lead to hurt and destruction. When it becomes the overriding reaction for every stress that comes your way, it crosses the line and becomes a stronghold that you want to work through.

REFLECT: Rate the ANGER: Circle my selection

Experience very little if at all   1   2   3   4   5   very much here

- Do I have any unhealthy anger surrounding the death of my loved one/s? If yes, in what ways? Write below:

- How has my anger hurt or destroyed relationships with others?

- How has my anger hurt or destroyed me?

- What does *Ephesians 4:26–27* say about anger?

Envy

Envy is the stronghold spoken of the least. Envy presents itself when you see other people doing things you won't be able to do now that your loved one is gone. Surrounding grief, most people don't even want to admit thinking envious thoughts, let alone letting those words come out of their mouth. You may think "It's not fair that your husband is living and mine is not," but there is no place to put this thought and associated emotions. But envy can be a very natural reaction to a loss; particularly when you recognize the full weight of all the secondary losses you have, and/or when that loss occurs outside of a natural or expected sequence.

It's important to realize that having some envy is normal. When you fall into the "it's not fair" trap, envy can become a stronghold. Not only is there envy, but guilt and shame can enter the picture and pile on top of it. Then this all-consuming envy can lead to bitterness, and the spiral downward continues. It may sound extreme, but if your "have-nots" are constantly being measured against someone else's "haves," you will want to examine envy as your stronghold.

REFLECT: Circle my selection

Rate the ENVY:

Experience very little if at all   1   2   3   4   5   very much here

- Am I measuring my "have-nots" against someone else's "haves"? In what way?

- What feelings of entitlement or anger do I notice when I am measuring my life against others?

- What does *1 Peter 2:1* say about envy?

Pride/Self-Sufficiency

Like anger, pride is another misunderstood and misidentified emotion. It is typically viewed as an outwardly boastful reaction that can be displayed by words that are said and actions displayed. But like anger, it is an internal response to loss shown in external ways. When it comes to grief, pride can manifest itself through withdrawal, outward strength, or even self-sufficiency. Self-sufficiency is a form of pride because it says, "I don't need help from anyone else. I can get through my grief on my own." This self-sufficiency is unwilling or even unable to ask for help. It can look like strength and stoicism. In the case of grief, the outside world is often relieved when someone seems to be doing just fine, so then your self-sufficiency is validated.

If a person has been raised in a family or culture where strength and stoicism are prized qualities and asking for help is a weakness, pride is most likely a stronghold.

REFLECT: Rate the PRIDE/SELF-SUFFICIENCY:

Experience very little if at all   1   2   3   4   5   very much here

- Am I hesitant or even unwilling to ask for help from others? If yes, write down a time this happened:

- In what ways do I see external or internal pride being an issue in my grief?

- What does *Proverbs 3:5–6* say about self-sufficiency?

Guilt/Regret/Shame

It is very common to struggle with these three ugly companions - guilt, regret, and shame — when a loved one dies. While similar, they are not the same.

Guilt: You have guilt when you did something that was in your control to stop. You have guilt about not doing something that was in your control to do.

Regret: Regret is when you may wish you did something different, but you had no control over the way things played out. You feel bad about something you did not cause or that was out of your control. Words like "would have, could have, should have, I wish" identify regret. Regret is when you try to take responsibility when there is none.

Shame: Shame attacks your personhood. You have negative thoughts about yourself and who you are. Guilt says, "I made a mistake." Shame says, "I am a mistake." Shame says words like "my loved one died because who I am was not enough for them."

The following is an example to help you see the differences: Your mother called and said that your father is dying and wishes to see you because he only has a couple days to live.

> Guilt response: For whatever reason, you intentionally decide to put off going to see him. By the time you get there, your father has passed. Because of the choice you made, you feel guilt for not seeing him before he died.

> Regret response: You make plans right away to see him. Your transportation gets delayed and you end up getting there later

than you expected. In the meantime, your father has passed. Because the delay was <u>beyond your control</u>, you feel regret for not seeing him before he died.

<u>Shame</u> response: For whatever reason, you think that he doesn't love or even like you as you are. You believe you are flawed and unworthy. By the time you get there, your father has passed. Because of your <u>negative thoughts about yourself</u>, you feel shame for not seeing him before he died.

Guilt v. regret v. shame. It is subtle, but the way you heal from them are different. It involves looking at your responsibility for your actions and changing how you look at the situation. Guilt says "I made a mistake" which brings conviction, a desire to change, and involves forgiveness. Regret says "I wish it was different, but I can't change what happened." Shame involves condemnation of who God made you to be. With God, seek the source of judgment. Is it from yourself, others, or do you think God is condemning you? Are you assuming something that is not accurate? Take it to God. He will make it clear.

Regardless of the cause of the death of your loved one/s, you are not to continue to bear the burden of guilt, regret, or shame.

REFLECT: Rate the GUILT: Circle my selection

Experience very little if at all   1   2   3   4   5   very much here

- How have I assumed guilt surrounding the death of my loved one/s?

- In what ways am I experiencing guilt? Write below:

- What does *1 John 3:20* say about guilt?

REFLECT: Rate the REGRET: Circle my selection

Experience very little if at all   1   2   3   4   5   very much here

- How have I assumed regret surrounding the death of my loved one/s?

- In what ways am I experiencing regret? Write below:

- What does *2 Corinthians 7:10* say about regret?

More about Shame

"There must be something wrong with me because after a year I am not over the death" or "I am worthless." You feel like no matter what you do, say, or think, you are not good enough. In grief, shame looks like you are blaming yourself. Shame is a silent disease that is unseen and epidemic. It is unseen because it is an inward feeling and epidemic because it is common and happens a lot.

Shame tells you that you can't express your true feelings because they are not right, besides no one wants to hear about your pain anyway. Shame is a feeling or thought that you are bad, wrong, stupid, to blame. It is anything that says you are not good enough or that you are weak.

When the circumstances of death (e.g. overdose, reckless/impaired driving, mental illness, suicide…) were a direct result of the deceased, your regret or guilt can turn to shame. It is not uncommon for you to assume a level of shame that would have belonged to the deceased, whether their actions were accidental or intentional. It sounds like this; "If I was just a little more…" or "why was I so dumb, naïve, an idiot…" God never intended for you to feel shame for another person's actions or sins. That includes past or present sin, repented or un-repented sin. You can start healing from shame by sitting with Jesus and pouring out all your true feelings to Him. Listen and let Him tell you who He says you are.

REFLECT: Rate the SHAME: Circle my selection

Experience very little if at all   1   2   3   4   5   very much here

- Have I assumed any unhealthy shame surrounding the death of my loved one? If yes, in what ways? Write below:

- In my shame, who is judging me?

- What does *Romans 8:1* say about judgment?

Sadness/Despair

Sadness comes when your heart is broken from loss. You will always feel moments of sadness to some degree, which is a healthy reminder that your heart loves deeply. God mourns your loss with you and desires to draw you near and comfort you.

Sometimes sadness turns into despair, a sense of hopelessness. For some people despair can be a serious stronghold. They have little to no experience with grief, healthy or otherwise, and may have the perception that the level of sadness should be in direct proportion to the depth of the loss. In your grief, you may think that your future happiness depends on you forgetting or abandoning the memory of your loved one/s. You think if you were to be happy without your loved one/s, it would diminish and disrespect the depth of relationship you had with them. These thoughts can lead to despair.

Despair comes when you do not believe your broken heart can or will be mended and you become hopeless about ever feeling joy again. These thoughts are what the enemy wants you to believe, to keep you stuck in despair. He will do anything to keep you in this state, to think that life will never be the same without your loved one/s. It is true that life will be different without your loved one/s, but that does not mean that your future life will be filled with misery. God's desire for your future is hope.

REFLECT: Rate the SADNESS/DESPAIR: Circle my selection

Experience very little if at all   1   2   3   4   5   very much here

- Have I assumed any despair surrounding the death of my loved one/s? If yes, what? Write below:

- Have I lost joy in life? If yes, write about the loss of hope and any distance from God.

- What does *Hebrews 6:18-19* say about despair and hope?

Fear/Worry/Anxiety

Fear, worry and anxiety are probably the most common strongholds in grief. These are rooted in the uncertainty of the future and the loss of control. When these happen, there is a tendency to change your vocabulary from possibly to probably to inevitably. You change to believing the worst and fearing everything. That is the combination that unlocks the door to fear, worry, and anxiety. You allow your worst-case scenarios to loop over and over until you think they will be your reality.

"I can't afford a mortgage so I am going to be homeless soon." When a concern is elevated to a place of fear, worry or anxiety it is no longer healthy and becomes a stronghold. Responses become exaggerated or unrealistic in relation to the actual situation. This leads a person to either over-react with regards to a decision or remain paralyzed in complete inaction for fear any decision may be the wrong decision.

Often the secondary losses discussed earlier can be a real cause of fear, worry or anxiety. These losses can reveal themselves over time. You need to manage these concerns and adjust to a new and different life after loss. This process is healthy and unfortunately necessary. Inability to function can become a stronghold.

REFLECT: Rate the FEAR/WORRY/ANXIETY: Circle my selection

Experience very little if at all   1   2   3   4   5   very much here

- Have I assumed any unhealthy fear surrounding the death of my loved one/s? If yes, what? Write below:

- What ways do I sense I am losing control?

- How have I overreacted to a situation or relationship?

- In what ways have I been so paralyzed with fear that I was unable to make a decision?

- In *1 Peter 5:7*, what am I to do with my fears?

Addiction

Some people have addictive personalities and, when stressed, will start or return to those behaviors as a way to cope with their loss. While it is common to think of addiction in the form of substance abuse, addiction can take many forms. For some it may manifest in the form of busyness such as working long hours in efforts to avoid coming home to an empty house. For others it may involve shopping or spending large amounts of money in an effort to fill the void left by the loss. Addiction may also manifest itself in the area of sex, rapidly changing or newly formed relationships. One of the most commonly ignored addictions is food, which can provide temporary comfort in grief, but may rapidly become an addiction, particularly since it is a seemingly endless supply after a loss. Any of these addictions are simply ways of avoiding the feelings of loss and filling the void with a substitute. But substitution, either with substance abuse, food, people or busyness, can never replace the person that died. You are called to do the hard work of grieving and let God mend your brokenness so that you can once again or maybe for the first time, be filled with joy.

REFLECT: Rate the ADDICTION: Circle my selection

Experience very little if at all   1   2   3   4   5   very much here

- Have I assumed any unhealthy addictions surrounding the death of my loved one/s? If yes, what? Write below:

- Are there previous addictions that have become more pronounced since the death of my loved one/s?

- What does *1 Corinthians 10:13* say about temptation?

Other Strongholds

You may think of other strongholds that are not listed. Take time to write them down. Remember, God knows you better than you know yourself. Be honest and let Him hold you in His strong love.

EXERCISE: IDENTIFYING STRONGHOLDS

PRAY: God, reveal strongholds that are keeping me from healing. Amen

REFLECT:
- What ways have I responded to loss in my past? (Look at my timeline from last chapter.)

- What were the strongholds and themes I identified from Chapter 5 and this chapter?

Anger	Envy	Pride
Guilt/Regret/Shame	Sadness/Despair	Addiction
Other _____		

- Look back in this chapter and see what I rated and wrote about each stronghold.

WRITE: Why do these have a strong hold on me?

PRAY: Lord, I come to You completely exposed. I tried to hide my brokenness from You. I tried to fix myself by turning towards sin and earthly strongholds as a glue to hold myself together. This has failed me because anything that is not of You eventually fails. No longer can I hide my cracks from You. You are the only Stronghold I need. When I don't have the words to pray, You hear my groans. Help me to be still, to listen, and to know that You alone are God. Amen

Thank God for all that He has taught you from the past and how He will use this past in your future. If these strongholds are keeping you so stuck you don't even know what to do, reach out to others for additional support.

MOVING FROM STUCK TO STRONG

In previous chapters, you went through a list of circumstances that make your grief journey unique to you. You looked at different thoughts and emotions examining what to do with them. It has been said that you can only heal what you feel. Carrying that one step further, you can only heal what you choose to reveal. That means getting messy with the reality of the loss and tackling some major strongholds that are holding you back from the life that God intends for you.

REFLECT: What must I remember in *2 Corinthians 4:8–9*?

God does not leave you trapped in your strongholds. He wants you to move from **STUCK TO STRONG**.

STUCK: Strongholds **T**hat **U**ndermine **C**hrist's **K**ingdom
    to   to
STRONG: Spirit **T**hat **R**elies **O**n **N**ever-failing **G**race

FIGURE 6.1

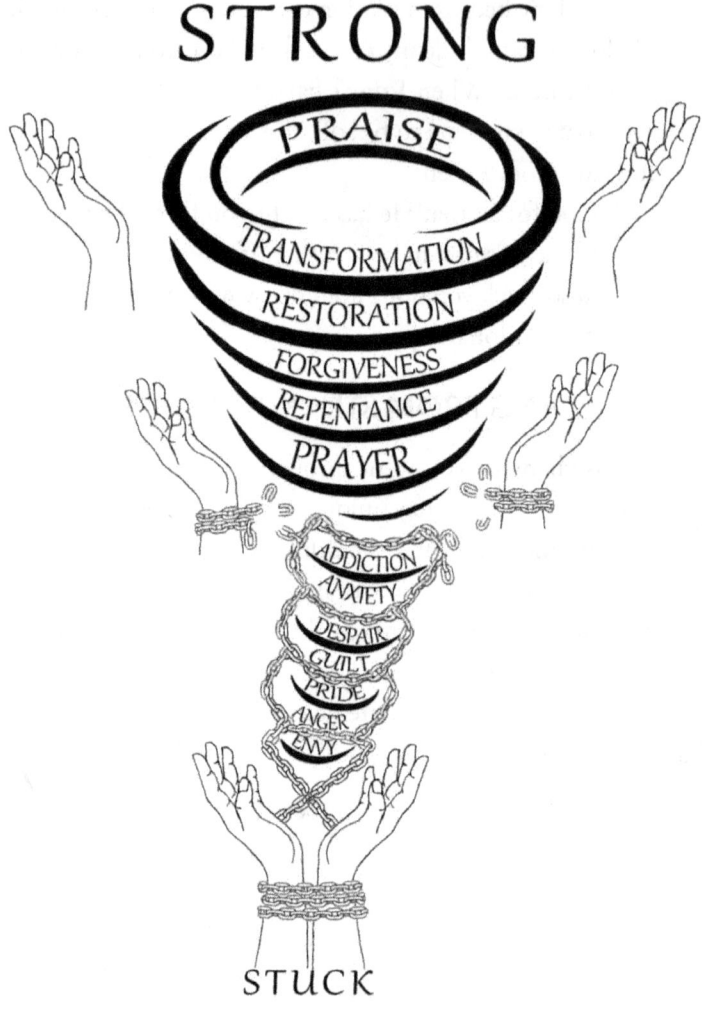

Source: Breyer, n.d.

Figure 6.1 illustrates how your strongholds keep you stuck and in bondage. The tighter you grip them, the tighter Satan's grip has on you. Relax and release your grip so you can reach out to God, <u>the</u> Lifeline, who is the only one who can truly mend your brokenness. You will find as you loosen your grip, your hands are available to open and lift up to God, beginning the process of becoming whole and **STRONG** (Spirit That Relies On Never-failing Grace).

The remaining chapters will discuss ways to release your strongholds and have God guide you forward.

FINAL THOUGHTS

Remember that strongholds begin as coping mechanisms. While they have common titles or categories, your strongholds are unique to you. Clinging to your strongholds can be an attempt to remove or distance yourself from your loss. It also can be a way to try to replace the loss or a way to hold onto your loved one/s.

There is an unspoken fear that if you let go of the guilt, anger, etc., you will lose your link to the one who died. But it is important to realize that releasing your strongholds and your grip on grief (or grief's grip on you) does not remove your link to your loved one. It allows you to retain the positive memories of them while at the same time becoming untethered from the chains that hold you back from an abundant life. The enemy desires you to be weak, but God desires you to be **STRONG** (Spirit That Relies On Never-failing Grace). God is for you!

Bible Verses

The Lord is my rock, my fortress and my deliverer; my God is my rock, in whom I take refuge, my shield and the horn of my salvation, my stronghold. Psalm 18:2

Be joyful always; pray continually; give thanks in all circumstances for this is God's will for you in Christ Jesus. 1 Thessalonians 5:16–18

CHAPTER 7

Change Direction
Seeing a New Wholeness of My Bowl

I called on your name, Lord, from the depths of the pit. You heard my plea: "Do not close your ears to my cry for relief." You came near when I called you, and you said, "Do not fear." Lamentations 3:55–57

In this chapter, the focus is more on God who heals, than on the broken bowl. This is a key to change - turning from where you were going and moving in a different direction. Repentance and forgiveness are also vitally important in your growth and change to be more Christ-like.

YOUR WILL, YOUR CHOICE

When a loved one dies, you are hurt. Questions about "why" can mingle with "who is responsible?" Hurt can be at the foundation of these emotions. If you aren't mindful, the hurt will fester becoming worse.

The chart below shows how unchecked hurt can escalate. Unhelpful thoughts and emotions pile on top of hurt and intensify. Now instead of being the one who was hurt, you become the one inflicting wounds on others.

TABLE 7:1

Hurt								
Hurt	Anger							
Hurt	Anger	Self-pity						
Hurt	Anger	Self-pity	Victim					
Hurt	Anger	Self-pity	Victim	Expansive Thinking				
Hurt	Anger	Self-pity	Victim	Expansive Thinking	Entitlement			
Hurt	Anger	Self-pity	Victim	Expansive Thinking	Entitlement	Bitter		
Hurt	Anger	Self-pity	Victim	Expansive Thinking	Entitlement	Bitter	Self righteous	
Hurt	Anger	Self-pity	Victim	Expansive Thinking	Entitlement	Bitter	Self righteous	Obsessed
Hurt	Anger	Self-pity	Victim	Expansive Thinking	Entitlement	Bitter	Self righteous	Obsessed	Revenge

Source: Roy, n.d.

REFLECT: Think about my grief/loss story. To help counter this hurt build up, consider the following:

- Where am I on the chart?

- Am I keeping a record of the ways I have been hurt by the death of my loved one?

- Am I keeping a record of the ways I have been hurt by others? In what ways?

- Do I have a right to expect justice or is my expectation solely what I want and think I deserve?

- How much of my energy, thought time, and conversation is taken up with inflicting wounds on others?

- Is there an imbalance of attention focused on me being right and/or on me being heard? If yes, in what ways?

- Am I negatively impacting others around me? How?

- Where is God in table 7:1?

It is not only bitterness and strongholds that keep you from grieving well, but sometimes you are stuck in grief because of your will. Your will is evident when you let your thoughts and ways be more important than God's ways. Your will is clearly seen when you push God away instead of letting him come close to you. Instead of putting all your energy on the anger and bitterness that can grow out of hurt, focus on Jesus and be grateful for all He is doing regardless of what you think or how it may feel. Go to God when it is just hurt you are experiencing. Let Him comfort you before it can grow out of control.

Consider the following essay derived from *Matthew 6:9–13*.

TABLE 7:2

I Cannot Pray (Author unknown)

I cannot pray "OUR," if my faith has no room for others and their need.

I cannot pray "FATHER," if I do not demonstrate this relationship to God in my daily living.

I cannot pray "WHO ART IN HEAVEN," if all of my interests and pursuits are in earthly things.

I cannot pray "HALLOWED BE THY NAME," if I am not striving for God's help to be holy.

I cannot pray "THY KINGDOM COME," if I am unwilling to accept God's rule in my life.

I cannot pray "THY WILL BE DONE," if I am unwilling or resentful of having it in my life.

I cannot pray "ON EARTH AS IT IS IN HEAVEN," unless I am truly ready to give myself to God's service here and now.

I cannot pray "GIVE US THIS DAY OUR DAILY BREAD," without expending honest effort for it or if I would withhold from my neighbor the bread I receive.

I cannot pray "FORGIVE US OUR TRESPASSES AS WE FORGIVE THOSE WHO TRESPASS AGAINST US," if I continue to harbor a grudge against anyone.

I cannot pray "LEAD US NOT INTO TEMPTATION," if I deliberately choose to remain in a situation where I am likely to be tempted.

I cannot pray "DELIVER US FROM EVIL," if I am not prepared to fight with my life and my prayer.

I cannot pray "THINE IS THE KINGDOM," if I am unwilling to obey the King.

I cannot pray "THINE IS THE POWER AND THE GLORY," if I am seeking power for myself and my own glory first.

I cannot pray "FOREVER AND EVER," if I am too anxious about each day's affairs.

I cannot pray "AMEN," unless I honestly say 'Not MY will, but THY will be done', so let it be.

It can seem impossible to pray. The ache of death still lingers and still hurts…a lot. God does not leave you in this place. Let His heart and will blend with yours. Let the Potter mold you, make you, form you, and repair your life bowl.

REPLACE THE URGE FOR REVENGE WITH REPENTANCE AND FORGIVENESS.

REPENTANCE

Repentance is when God's will and your will become one. It is taking a self-inventory by asking yourself the following: What am I holding onto that I need to let go? Repentance is agreeing with God that you have chosen your way over His way. It is turning towards God and letting Him take care of your life. Repentance is turning 180° from a current action or belief and "walking" in a different direction towards God. It's the process that God created to move you towards spiritual maturity.

REFLECT: In the Bible, repentance means to "change one's mind." This starts a new way of believing and acting. What does the Bible say about change?

- *John 8:3-11:*

- Read *2 Corinthians 7:10*. What does this verse mean? How can I apply it to my grief?

What do repentance and distress have to do with your grief? The Bible says to stop trying to fix yourself or fix the reasons your loved one died. Stop blaming others or yourself. These thoughts and actions keep you dependent on yourself to gain control instead of dependent on God to change you. When you take charge trying to determine future outcomes, you put yourself as god on the throne of your life.

REFLECT: See what the Bible says about "self" focus:

- In *Ezekiel 28:2*

- In *Job 12:13*

Adjust your focus and turn your life TO God. Look to the God who holds your bowl of emotions and grief.

EXERCISE: REPENTANCE

RUN TO GOD. He is my Father and He wants me to come to Him:

- In *Matthew 11:29* what does God say He will do if I come to Him?

- Who does God say He is in *Psalm 68:5*?

- Who does God say I am in *2 Corinthians 6:18*?

TELL HIM ALL ABOUT IT. God wants me to tell him what I am thinking and feeling:

- Look at the timeline and strongholds from previous chapters and write down something that I want to tell God I want to repent of, to change and to grow closer to Him:

GIVE MY BOWL TO HIM. Surrender my life. Let go. Change my focus and direction to Jesus. This is repentance. This means that I do not intend to keep repeating the same thoughts and actions. I must be real. I may have fear associated with "letting go" of my loved one/s. Letting go does not mean that I am forgetting them. It just means that I am not keeping control of my feelings, thoughts and actions. I am putting my life, my trust, and my loved one/s in His hands.

- What does it say in *1 John 1:9* about confessing my sins?

PRAY: Father, I repent of _____. I do not want this in my life anymore and in Jesus name, I command it to leave my soul. I plead the blood of Christ over this sin, this rebellion against You. Wash me clean; renew me. O Father make me holy through and through right here, in this. I invite the Holy Spirit to come and live in the exact place. Whatever was confessed, wherever a lie lives, I ask the Holy Spirit to go there. Thank You for giving me faith to take this step. Amen

Final Thoughts On Repentance

Focusing on God does not deny that your loved one has died. It still seeps through cracks into your emotions and life every day. When you obsess on the death and turn your back on God, the Holy Spirit will quicken in you. When this happens you can repent, turn, and offer your bowl to God.

Being "all about God" and not as consumed in the death takes time and intent. Remember you can talk with God anywhere (in your car, in the elevator, to yourself, in a meeting, sitting in your family room etc.). Run to God quickly when you are overwhelmed with emotion. You will experience the freedom that it brings! Friends, holiness is yours when you ask for it, seek it, and pursue it. God repairs your broken places.

…for though the righteous fall seven times, they rise again…
Proverbs 24:16

He will cover you with his feathers, and under his wings you will find refuge; his faithfulness will be your shield and rampart.
Psalm 91:4

FORGIVENESS: MENDING MY BOWL

Bear with each other and forgive one another if any of you has a grievance against someone. Forgive as the Lord forgave you.
Colossians 3:13

Forgiveness is a major key in healing and wholeness, especially of relationships. Unforgiveness is bondage and restricts us from participating fully in life.

Forgiveness IS:
- Freedom
- An internal process
- Primarily for you

- Takes time and hard work
- Trusting God for justice, to remedy your pain
- Releasing yourself from a burden
- Necessary for your spiritual, emotional and physical well-being
- The nature of God
- A "learned" action
- Giving the other person grace
- A gentle process with the help of the Holy Spirit
- A gift from God
- Your decision

Other_____

Forgiveness is NOT:
- Excusing the wrong
- Agreeing to more of the same treatment
- Deciding what was done was "not so bad" (denial or minimizing)
- Letting others off the hook
- Pardoning what the other person did
- An emotion
- Forgetting
- The same as reconciliation
- Placing guilt on the other person
- Fixing the other person

Other_____

Why Forgive

Unforgiveness keeps pain and bitterness in your life bowl. It leaks out through the cracks and flows out over the rim. Unforgiveness can preoccupy you. Remember repentance? You have decided to place your focus and change your direction to be about Jesus. Jesus taught and demonstrated forgiveness. Now it's your turn.

REFLECT: See what the following Bible verses have to say about forgiveness:

- *2 Corinthians 2:10–11a*

- *Ephesians 4:30–32*

- *Mark 11:25*

Forgiveness is an action and not a feeling. How many times do you hear people say, "I can't forgive him, I don't feel it"? How many times have you said this? Most of the time, you won't "feel" like forgiving. It's important to recognize that this is not about judging yourself or hurting yourself more. The goal is to be in relationship with God and through Him, forgive whoever has hurt you so you can move towards healing and wholeness of that relationship. You just have to choose to do it and the feelings will follow.

Unforgiveness breeds resentment and anger. It is one of Satan's tools that he uses to destroy relationships. Forgiveness is a process which begins with a choice and a willingness to act. As you take the first step towards forgiveness, God will comfort and empower you to complete the action. You may need to forgive someone for what they did or for something they did not do. For example, "I forgive you for not attending school events".

WHO TO FORGIVE

Who do you need to seek forgiveness from? Whose bowl have you cracked? Ask God to show and reveal to you who you need to forgive.

REFLECT: I want to answer the following questions to help me discover who I need to forgive:

- Who has hurt me knowingly or unknowingly?

- Is there anyone who I hold a grudge against? Is there anyone towards whom I have resentment?

- Is there anyone I hate?

- Do I want to be reconciled with anyone?

- Do I want God to forgive me?

- Do I want to ask forgiveness from emotions I have towards God?

What About Forgiving Yourself

There may be some things that you regret doing or saying. You may think you need to forgive yourself. Actually, you can't really do that because forgiveness takes at least two people. One to ask for forgiveness and one to forgive. You can't ask for forgiveness from yourself and also give yourself forgiveness. You can ask God for forgiveness. He will always forgive you. Instead of saying, "I need to forgive myself", say "I'm not going to carry this any longer. God forgive me."

By doing this, you will receive God's gift of forgiveness.

EXERCISE: FORGIVENESS LETTER
HOW TO FORGIVE

Right now, I am going to take time with God. He knows me better than I know myself. I am going to pour out all that is in my bowl and write about the who, what, and when. This process of writing is so I can get it all out, expose it to the light, and place it on God's altar for Him to burn it off of me.

PRAY: Dear Heavenly Father, I thank you for the riches of Your kindness, perseverance, and patience towards me, knowing that Your kindness has led me to repentance. I confess that I have not shown that same kindness and patience towards those who have hurt or offended me. Instead, I have held on to my anger, bitterness, resentment and hurt towards them, especially the hurt. Please bring to my mind all the people I need to forgive in order that I may now do so. In Jesus' name I pray. Amen

REMEMBER: Recall what has happened to help me write this letter

- From the previous "Who to Forgive" Reflect section, write below the people I listed

- Recall anything that is a crack in my bowl that is related to my loss. Make a list in the space below:

- Are there strongholds, bitterness and/or anything on my timeline in chapter 5 & 6 that illustrates a lack of forgiveness?

WRITE: Now just start writing. Do this in a journal to give myself enough space to pour "my guts" out. Writing a letter to God about the people and/or items on my list will help express my real emotions to God. He can take whatever I give Him. This letter does not need to be grammatically correct, nor be complete sentences.

Forgiveness Prayers

Now that all is in the open before the glory of God, it is time to pray to God for forgiveness. For each item on the list (from REMEMBER section above), handwrite a separate forgiveness prayer. You can use what is below as a guide. If there is a person you need to forgive, insert their name in the blank spaces. Now speak the prayer out loud:

Lord Jesus, as I have been forgiven, I now choose to forgive _____ for what was done or left undone. I release my offenses with _____ to God. I resign my "right" to seek revenge. I choose not to hold on to my resentment. I ask You to heal my damaged emotions. Thank you for setting me free from the bondage of my bitterness. I now ask You to bless those who have hurt me. In Jesus' name, Amen

REFLECT: What does the following have to say about forgiveness?

- *Matthew 6:14–15*

FINAL THOUGHTS

Repentance is something YOU DO to come closer to God. Forgiveness is an initial and important step in order to truly give it to God. Forgiveness is something GOD DOES FOR YOU to come closer to Him. Having taken the steps to repent and forgive, you are putting your bowl back together piece by piece, though not by your own strength but with God's strength.

God gathers the pieces of your broken bowl close to His heart. He lovingly aligns the pieces back together. He touches the edges. He places each shard exactly where it will complete the repairs. He sees, He touches, He feels the bowl. He is intimately close. His breath falls upon it. The bowl is together, yet it will not be as it was before. He makes it even more beautiful than before it was broken. The bowl is your life.

Bible Verses

As far as the east is from the west, so far has he removed our transgressions from us. Psalm 103:12

…God's kindness is intended to lead you to repentance… Romans 2:4

I am writing to you, dear children, because your sins have been forgiven on account of his name. 1 John 2:12

CHAPTER 8

Integrating Loss
Glue of Recovery

*For in him all things were created: things in heaven and on earth, visible and invisible, whether thrones or powers or rulers or authorities; all things have been created through him and for him. He is before all things, **and in him all things hold together**. Colossians 1:16–17*

In the previous chapter, repentance and forgiveness were discussed and practiced so that God can start to fill the cracks of your bowl. This chapter will continue filling in your bowl with God's "glue" by looking at ways your loss can be integrated in your life. Your participation in this process is to focus on the LOVE that God has for you and to cooperate with Him.

REFLECT: Earlier chapters looked at different aspects of loss; the actual loss, the secondary losses, and other lifetime losses. Loss is not a one-time event. It carries over to other places in life.

Look back at earlier identified losses and if others come to mind, write them below:

Listing your losses is not meant to keep you there in the loss, it is for you to recognize them and integrate God's promises in with them.

INTEGRATING LOSS…

How do you make the loss a part of your life? There is no easy answer for this, though a significant part of it is putting God first and in the forefront of your life. Put God first. Instead of holding on tightly to your loved one/s and what happened, place them in His hands. Let Him love you by giving them to Him. Placing them with God is the most loving thing you can do. By this action, God will give you hope and trust in Him.

…Through Hope

Most of the glue of God is still wet because it is mixed with your tears. At this point, you can't see that the glue is in place to hold you together. Life without is still…life without. You need hope.

Know that you are not defined by your circumstances. You are not perfect, though you are being perfected. This is the hope for every follower of Jesus. Hope is the joyful anticipation of good.

REFLECT: How can I integrate my loss in hopeful, positive and healthy ways?

- First, I want to <u>know</u> who God is. I want to read scripture to know who He says He is, not who I think He is.
  - Read *Lamentation 3:19-26* and write down who God is:

- Next, I want to <u>experience</u> who God is. Being able to draw on my personal encounters with God helps make Him real. When I sense God in my life, my head knowledge and thoughts about God travels to my heart where I can feel Him in a new and more complete way.
  - Write down some of my experiences with God below. Include experiences that happened while dealing with

and after my loss. NOTE: If you are new in a relationship with God, you may not have history with Him. Ask others you know that speak of their lives with Christ to tell you some of their experiences with God. Make notes of their stories. Soon you will have your own.

If you rely on other people to meet all your needs and desires, they will certainly fail you. Realize that God is MORE THAN enough for you. Commit to seek the truth of God and that HE WILL meet all your needs.

...Through Trust

You may be thinking, "I can't go on." No, you can't — without Jesus.

According to the dictionary, trust means a "firm belief in the reliability or strength of someone or something" (Trust, n.d.). Who or what do you put your firm belief in?

Think about a chair. You can talk about the chair; how solid it looks and what you will use it for. But if you never actually sit on it, you can't really trust that the chair will hold you. Trust is when you sit and put your full weight on the chair. If you are not willing to put your full weight on the chair, what is the point of sitting down at all? You don't trust the chair. Sitting on the edge is uncomfortable because you are straining your back and legs to balance. You may have a break from standing but in the end, you may have more pain.

Carrying this one step further, there is a difference between sitting on a chair (functional support) and sitting in a chair (relational and emotional support). When you sit on a chair, it holds you. When you sit in a chair, it gives you rest. The one you sit in is the comfy chair you sink into after a long hard day. This is your favorite chair, the one you would curl up in and ignore the rest of the world if you could. The tensions of the day fade away.

The chair you sit <u>on</u> is like the busyness of the world. You take short breaks in your schedule, get restored and then move on to the next thing. The chair you sit <u>in</u> is like the Lord. When you place your full trust <u>in</u> the Lord, you will truly find rest!

REFLECT: Read the following scriptures to know Jesus' character and His names. Write responses next to the scripture:

- *Matthew 1:22–23*

- *John 8:12*

- *John 6:48–51*

- *Isaiah 9:6*

- *John 1:14*

- *Revelation 22:16*

- *Revelation 22:13*

- *Philippians 2:9–11*

- Which one of Jesus' character or name is the most meaningful to me? Why?

Proverbs 3:5. says, *"Trust in the Lord with all your heart and lean not on your own understanding."* Place your trust in Jesus and don't depend on yourself.

- What does it mean for me to trust in Jesus? Write my thoughts below:

- In what ways will I focus on Jesus and give Him my bowl?

Many times when there have been trials in life, you have learned to depend only on yourself. "Watch out for #1. Pull yourself up by your bootstraps. Stand on your own two feet." Living a life of trust is to unlearn a life of self-dependence. Living a life of trusting Him means to learn a life of God-dependence. It is a life of laying aside your own plans and expectations and surrender to His. Now that you trust Him or are moving towards trusting Him, your strongholds will lessen until they have no control over you.

Remember your strongholds? A stronghold is anything that you trust more than God. You have repented from them. They no longer control you because you have put your trust in God instead of the other things and people that kept you in bondage.

DESCRIPTIONS OF GLUE

How does glue work? It is the perfect combination of materials working in perfect union to cause the bonding to take place.

Glue:
- Bonds the broken pieces together
- Has to flow and spread to what it is being applied
- Has to come in physical contact with what it is being bonded
- Can be used to bind things together or to keep things out
- Is sticky when wet, but hardens when it dries
- Needs to set
- Must be dry to reach its significant strength and sometimes the object being glued has to be clamped to hold it in place
- Comes in different forms and types depending on what is broken
- As a strong bond is sturdier and more resilient than the material being glued

You try to repair brokenness with a universal white glue. It may work ok, though rarely is it the best glue to use. With the universal white glue, you will settle for good enough hoping the repair holds or you may treat the item gingerly and not use it to its full potential. Your broken thing is not what it was before.

When a chemist formulates glue, he starts by looking at the materials that need to be put back together. He knows that although circumstances may be similar, not all glues work in all situations. Is it a hard or soft surface? Is that surface porous like stone or impermeable like steel? The chemist then evaluates the environment in which the glue will be used. A hot glue gun is not used for something exposed to heat. Waterproof glue is used in a shower. Each application is unique and the glue often needs to be customized for the set of materials and environments it will be used in. The same can be said for you. You are uniquely broken with your own set of circumstances. The environment you are called to survive and thrive in is also unique.

God is the great Chemist. He is lovingly, carefully, and personally formulating a glue that is perfect for you. A glue that will make you whole and stronger than you were before. A glue to last an eternity.

EXERCISE: GOD IS THE GLUE

Look back to the scripture at the beginning of this chapter. It doesn't say that I hold all things together but that HE does.

The apostle Paul went through many trials and pain. In *2 Corinthians 12:7–10* he endures a "thorn in his flesh" and still boasts about the sufferings he endured because of his faith in Jesus Christ. When I am weak, He is strong. God is the glue!

SCRIPTURE: Take a look at scripture to see the ways that God is the glue. Write my responses below:

- What does God say about my needs in *Philippians 4:19*

- Read how Jesus glues my cracks and make them more beautiful:
  - *2 Corinthians 9:8*

  - *Ephesians 1:10*

  - *Philippians 4:13*

MEDITATE: Look back at the descriptions of glue and translate them to ways that Jesus can be the glue in my life. Journal my thoughts below:

WRITE: Now that God is the glue, how does this change the way I live with grief?

The following is an example of one person's response:

FIGURE 8.1: GOD IS THE GLUE

How can Jesus be the glue in my life?

By protecting and strengthening me: He glues the tiny cracks (like pride, busyness, selfishness...) before they grow bigger and perhaps even before I know about them

By identifying the kind of glue I need: He knows the trials I have faced and will face. He knows what I will need to keep me strong and give me faith to endure any battle I will face

By giving the right amount: He knows how much "Jesus Glue" I need in the private places inside me and also my public places (my words, actions, behaviors...). He gives the right amount at the right time

By knowing how long the glue needs to set: How much I need to rest, meditate, pray, and be quiet to heal

By directing my life: He "clamps" (stops and directs) me for my best living

By knowing how to join the pieces of my life back together: He bonds my large and small pieces in the way He has designed me

Now that God is the glue, how does this change the way I live with grief?

I choose to see what God has for me every day

I let go of the broken pieces that are keeping me stuck (anger, guilt, shame disappointments...) and actively turn them over to God. I no longer need to hold on to them

No regrets, guilt, or shame about my past. I can accept who I am trusting God will bring out only what I need to remember, making today better according to His plan for me

I learn to love unconditionally, know that God will teach me, and provide opportunities to love others. He will hold me

I rest in Him

Now that the glue is in place, it becomes tacky, beginning to hold my pieces in place. It is not by my effort that this happens, because if it were, the pieces may hold for a moment then fall apart again. My glue is temporary. God's glue is eternal and everlasting.

BELIEVING THE PROMISE

As you spend time here on earth, you make the choice to hope in and trust God in the midst of your trials and pain remembering that God did not cause the bad, but through it, He will use it for good.

Jesus said, "...*I am the resurrection and the life. The one who believes in me will live, even though they die; and whoever lives by believing in me will never die....*" *John 11:25–26*. Believing in Christ for the forgiveness of sins and the promise of eternal life in Him is essential to your healing. The God of all comfort is familiar with your suffering and will walk with you through the toughest days of your grief journey, offering comfort for today and hope for the future.

- Read *Galatians 2:20*. How did the apostle Paul state his new identity and purpose? Write your response below:

REFLECT: I have a new identity and purpose. Insert my name in the blanks and read out loud:

- Christ's death on the cross paid _____'s way to new life in Him.
- God sees _____ without sin because Christ gave His life to pay for _____'s sins.
- _____ can approach the throne of grace, into resurrected life, to be with God forever.

With confidence and assurance, you can believe and proclaim that His power is made perfect in weakness. His grace IS sufficient. Jesus loves you WITH your bowl of loss. He will never leave you nor forsake you. Your weaknesses allow Christ to be your strength!

PRAY: Heavenly Father, I praise you! I am starting to understand Your plan for my life. Yes, I have suffered a loss, and on this side of heaven, You know it hurts. Death was never a part of Your original plan, but You overcame death by sending Your Son to walk the same path of suffering that I am walking right now. Because of this, I have hope. The life You desire for me is not one of brokenness, but one of wholeness through trust and hope. Fill every crack in me with Your glue, knowing that I will be stronger with You. In Jesus' name I pray. Amen

FINAL THOUGHTS

What does it mean for God to be the glue? In the broken and cracked places in your life, He is what joins your pieces together to make your life whole. It is not by your effort that this happens, it is all by God's grace. All you have to do is allow Him to do this for you.

Jesus promises that there is more to life than what you can see, feel, or touch. There is eternal life with Him to those that believe in Him. There is mortality and there is life, not death. He has conquered death and you will live with Him. You can hold tightly to this truth. When you understand and believe this promise, you can grieve with hope, not despair. You can trust God in everything. You have a God who loves and cares for you deeply in the midst of your pain.

Give your loved one/s to Jesus, knowing that He is with you to comfort and pave the way for a newly, integrated life in Him.

He is your strength and your refuge. He is GLUED to you and you are glued to Him!

Bible Verses

Where can I go from your Spirit? Where can I flee from your presence? If I go up to the heavens, you are there; if I make my bed in the depths, you are there. If I rise on the wings of the dawn, if I settle on the far side of the sea, even there your hand will guide me, your right hand will hold me fast. Psalm 139:7-10

But we have this treasure in jars of clay to show that this all-surpassing power is from God and not from us. We are hard pressed on every side, but not crushed; perplexed, but not in despair; persecuted, but not abandoned; struck down, but not destroyed. 2 Corinthians 4:7-9

CHAPTER 9
Transformation
GOLD Glue

Create in me a pure heart, O God, and renew a steadfast spirit within me. Psalm 51:10

Last chapter, you discovered ways to integrate your loss in your present life. The essential way to do this is to give your loss to Jesus and let God glue your bowl back together. This chapter looks at the lessons you have learned through this grief journey and how you can have a transformed life.

LESSONS LEARNED

Throughout this workbook, you have learned much, you have felt various emotions, and you have changed. You have grown since your grief experience.

The following are some lessons you have learned:

Your Grief Story is Your Grief Story

- Your loss is unique to you because your life and story are different than others
- Your story is unique to you. You can take the time to reconcile the death with your life and how to move forward
- The emotions you experience are varied. All of us experience them at different times and in various intensities
- There are many factors that contribute to your grief

- Your secondary losses can influence your grieving as much as the actual loss

God is Your Comfort and Strength

- As you express your emotions, let God be your rock
- Everything is in God's time, not yours
- With your loved one gone, you realize you are not in control. That's when you surrender all to God and acknowledge that you can't do anything on your own
- Place your trust in God to comfort and heal you
- God does not leave you in your grief, He walks beside you and directs you through it
- Strongholds can keep you stuck in grief. Letting go of your strongholds does not mean you are letting go of your love one/s. **Let God be your Stronghold**

God Uses Your Bowl for Good

- You don't always understand why God allows bad things to happen, but you do know that good things can come out of it
- Eventually you understand that God wants more for you than just sadness
- As you heal, you grow
- Learn from the loss. Acknowledge and improve your living relationships
- Grief is a continual process with some days better than others. God will use all your days for His goodness and glory
- God transforms your bowl into something more beautiful than it was before

- God is your Glue. He joins your pieces together to make your life whole
- Other lessons learned

REFLECT: It can be helpful to look back to where I was when I started this journey. The reason I do this is not to transport myself back to the past, but to glimpse back at my past to measure how far I have traveled.

- I want to take a moment to remember my thoughts, emotions, strongholds, etc. when I opened this workbook. Write them out below:

- How has my heart been renewed? Look back at the chapters and/or journal entries to see how my heart has changed. Write it out:

If you are healing through this workbook on your own, now is the time to open the envelope from chapter 1. On this index card you wrote what your purpose is for doing this workbook. Share this with your trusted friend.

TRANSFORMATION

Transformation is defined as "the act of changing in character or condition" (Transformation, n.d.). First of all, transformation is an action. It is something you have to <u>choose</u> to do. It also involves change — change from who you were to who you want to be. God's transformation is Him changing you to reflect His character and His ways.

REFLECT: Instead of looking at my loss as a loss, stop and look at the blessings that have occurred because of this loss. Changing the way I look at my loss can be transforming.

- Quiet myself with God
- Say: God, help me to see that You will make a way for me
- Look through this workbook
- Ask God to bring to mind the following instances since my loved one died:
  - Encouragement
  - Care
  - Miracle
  - Renewal
  - New experiences
- Now make a blessing list

- I can add to this list as I move forward

Transformation Takes Time

Transformation is something that is ongoing and takes time. Give yourself grace in this area. Time:

- Is God's gift
- Keeps you from getting stuck in the past
- Gives you a fresh start
- Allows a chance to amend your ways

- Does heal all wounds
- Is where God is, at the beginning and at the end
    There is a time for everything, and a season for every activity under the heavens: Ecclesiastes 3:1

Transformation is Living Your Life in a New Way

REFLECT: Read the following and circle the ones that will be your new goals after this group or study:

- Living through my grief will mean saying goodbye to life as it once was
- Living will involve my mind, my emotions and my God
- Living involves releasing it all to God
- Living means committing to cease trying to make the past a part of my present
- Living means choosing to look at the facts and be at peace with the memories
- Living means relegating the past to the past
- Living means letting it go and leaving it there
- Living means putting Jesus at the center of my life
- Living means going about one day at a time
- Living means saying goodbye to the daily impact of the past
- Living means saying goodbye to the daily pain
- Living means verbally stating that I will not live in the past
- Living does not mean forgetting
- Living means I have present needs that God plans to meet in new ways
- Living means expecting God to show up every minute/hour/day/week & forever

- Living means asking God to meet my every need
- Living means thanking God for all the ways He has, does, and will bless me
- Living means actively watching for God's move on my life
- Living is knowing God has a plan for me
- Living means God will use all of my life for His glory
- I will live by faith in Jesus Christ
- I will not live by seeing the world by my own narrow viewpoint
- I will live daily with God filling the empty places in my life
- I will live by trusting daily in God's love for me

*<u>From the list above, underline the one you will incorporate into your daily life now. (You will write down this goal in the EXERCISE section later in this chapter)</u>

PRAY: Dear Lord, please carve away all that is not pure in my heart. I ask You to dwell in my heart — a heart that may be crowded — and swell within me. Create in me a pure heart, oh God, and renew a right spirit within me. I ask that You align my priorities with Yours. Heal my heart of suffering and transform me in the power of Your Holy Spirit. Amen

Living Well

Living well with your grief means focusing on what matters most.

REFLECT: Circle the items that apply to you now:

- I will seek God's eyes to view my family and friends as He sees them

- Family and friends are important. I will reach out to others asking for support
- Family and friends are important. I will reach out and love them, offering support
- Family and friends are important. I will share about my loved one/s
- Family and friends are important. I will listen as they share in their own way about the deceased
- God is important. I join or renew my participation with His church/His community as He leads me
- Jesus is important. I will devote time to be with Him through prayer, worship, and learning through His Word, the Bible
- I will seek a heartfelt, soul relationship with Jesus
- I will seek God's special design for my life
- I will seek God to understand how He uses suffering to help me grow
- I will endeavor to understand that joy and pain can co-exist
- As God leads me, I will share with others that He has focused me on HOW to live instead of being stuck in the WHY of death
- I will grow from the pain and brokenness allowing for time as I need it
- I will count my blessings and praise God daily for them

*From the list above, underline the one that you will add as a goal going forward. (You will write down this goal in the EXERCISE section later in this chapter)

GOLD AND GOD

Kintsukuroi: the art of repairing broken pottery using gold to glue the pieces together

You: broken from your loss, looking for a way to heal

God: the Gluer who wants to repair your broken loss, putting you together not as you once were, but in an even more beautiful way. The Gold that glues your brokenness together is The Master Artist, God

> *For we are God's masterpiece. He has created us anew in Christ Jesus...Ephesians 2:10 (NLT)*

Gold is:

- Valuable
- Bright
- Ductile/Workable
- A conductor of electricity
- A conduit of heat
- A "noble" metal, meaning it stands apart from other metals because it barely reacts with other elements
- Resistant to most acids

Your bowl was broken, but with gold running throughout it now, it is more beautiful than it was before it was broken. God is the gold, which holds your bowl together.

In many ways, God is like gold.

God is:

- Valuable — Worthy is the Lamb
- Bright — The light of the world
- Workable — Works for the good of those who love him

- Power — Mighty God, Everlasting Father
- Passionate — Love comes from Him
- Magnificent — He is the one true God
- Constant — The same yesterday, today and forever
- With God in your life, you can "*resist the devil, and he will flee from you.*" James 4:7

REFLECT:

- How have I seen God transform me in these chapters?

- In what ways have I seen the pure love God has for me?

- In what ways do I see how constant and solid my God is?

When you are transformed and made new, the response to God is to worship Him. Be joyful, declaring the following Psalm aloud:

Sing to the Lord a new song; sing to the Lord, all the earth.
Sing to the Lord, praise his name; proclaim
his salvation day after day.
Declare his glory among the nations, his
marvelous deeds among all peoples.
For great is the Lord and most worthy of praise;
he is to be feared above all gods.

> For all the gods of the nations are idols, but
> the Lord made the heavens.
>
> Splendor and majesty are before him; strength
> and glory are in his sanctuary.
>
> Ascribe to the Lord, all you families of nations,
> ascribe to the Lord glory and strength.
>
> Ascribe to the Lord the glory due his name; bring
> an offering and come into his courts.
>
> Worship the Lord in the splendor of his holiness;
> tremble before him, all the earth.
>
> Say among the nations, "The Lord reigns." The world is firmly established, it cannot be moved; he will judge the peoples with equity. Let the heavens rejoice, let the earth be glad; let the sea resound, and all that is in it. Let the fields be jubilant, and everything in them; let all the trees of the forest sing for joy. Let all creation rejoice before the Lord, for he comes, he comes to judge the earth. He will judge the world in righteousness and the peoples in his faithfulness.
>
> Psalm 96

EXERCISE: TRANSFORMED LIFE — GOLD

Throughout this workbook, I may have asked; "How could this loss change my life for the better?" "How could I think about life without my loved one/s?" Bad things do happen to good people because of this fallen world but God does not want me to stay in that same place. The Lord wants me to place my entire hope and trust in Him alone. His plan for me is to live a life that is transformed inside and out.

SCRIPTURE: Read the following scriptures and write down ways I can live transformed:

- *Matthew 6:33*

- *Philippians 4:6*

- *2 Peter 1:3*

- *Proverbs 16:3*

- *Romans 12:2*

WRITE: Earlier in the chapter I looked in the sections "TRANSFORMATION IS LIVING YOUR LIFE IN A NEW WAY" and "LIVING WELL" and underlined "new things" I can incorporate into my life now and going forward. Write them down here:

MEDITATE: Live in the now. I now tell God the "new things" I am going to incorporate into my life. Not only do I want to talk about a transformed life, but I want to live a transformed life so my beliefs become my actions.

WRITE: God has a plan for my life. He wants to give me a new life that is actually simple (though simple is not the same as easy) — to have Jesus in the center every day. I want to live in a new way, focusing on Jesus, reflecting His character within and then expressing it outwardly.

Consider my "new things" I just wrote above. Think about them as I respond to the following questions:

- What area/s in my life does God want me to change to become more like Him? (For example, I underlined "Living involves releasing it all to God" because I am critical of others and I tend to judge them. A response may be, "God wants me to see others as He does – with love and grace because He is the only true judge.") Write down my response below:

- How can I start to live the life that God now has for me? Write down a specific and tangible action I can take. (e.g. God wants me to get in contact with my mom and apologize to her for judging her and being angry with her).

ACTION: Tell someone else about what I want to change to become more Christ-like in character. Let them know about my specific action plan. That will help me live the life that God has for me now. Have this person check in with me at a later date to see how I am doing with it.

KNOW: This is an activity you may have to revisit several times as you move along in your grief process.

FINAL THOUGHTS

When you think you can't go on another day, you can because there is *"incomparably great power for us who believe...." Ephesians 1:19.* Declaring that Christ is enough, and realizing you are enough because of Christ, is the absolute key in conquering your battles. With confidence and assurance, you believe and shout out that His power is made perfect in weakness. His grace IS enough!

You can only imagine the extraordinary and pleasing life He wants to give you — an eternal life free from human limitations and disappointments, weaknesses and suffering. Pain, disappointment, and death will be no more.

Jesus is the Gold who holds you now. He has shaped your gold-touched bowl of life. God <u>has</u> overcome your loss from death!

Bible Verses

If I say, "Surely the darkness will hide me and the light become night around me," even the darkness will not be dark to you; the night will shine like the day, for the darkness is as light to you. Psalm 139:11–12

Not only so, but we also glory in our sufferings, because we know that suffering produces perseverance; perseverance, character; character, hope. And hope does not put us to shame, because God's love has been poured out into our hearts through the Holy Spirit, who has been given to us. Romans 5:3–5

Therefore, as God's chosen people, holy and dearly loved, clothe yourselves with compassion, kindness, humility, gentleness and patience. Colossians 3:12

Come, you who are blessed by my Father; take your inheritance, the kingdom prepared for you since the creation of the world. Matthew 25:34

He will wipe every tear from their eyes. There will be no more mourning or crying or pain, for the old order of things has passed away. Revelation 21:4

CHAPTER 10

Something To Celebrate
In the Artist's Gallery of Life

Everyone will share the story of your wonderful goodness; they will sing with joy about your righteousness. Psalm 145:7 (NLT)

Now it is time to honor God and the ways He has led you to relational, spiritual and emotional healing through the G.O.L.D. workbook.

Consider:

- Honoring God in worship and celebration
- Reflecting on the life of deceased loved one/s
- Receiving a degree of closure regarding the loss of loved one/s

You may wish to design a service with these considerations:

- Have an intimate gathering
  - Who would you like to invite? Just a special person or two?
- Write down a Bible verse and/or song you would like included
  - If you have chosen a Bible verse, consider being the one to read it out loud

- Write words that defeat the strongholds you identified in Chapter 6. Select antonyms and/or Fruit of the Spirit (*Galatians 5:22*) that defeat them
- Share something about your loved one
  - Bring an item and/or picture that has a cherished memory attached to it

Other ideas:

- Have a balloon release
- Raise funds for a cause you or your loved one cares about
- Provide a meal to someone less fortunate
- Have a casual gathering of special people to tell stories about your loved one

These are just a few suggestions. You will have other ideas that are unique; just like you, your story, and now your celebration.

Following are some good verses to pray and consider at this time:

- *Whatever is true, whatever is noble, whatever is right, whatever is pure, whatever is lovely, whatever is admirable; if anything is excellent or praiseworthy, think of such things. Philippians 4:8*
- *For I know the plans I have for you, declares the Lord, plans to prosper you and not to harm you, plans to give you hope and a future. Jeremiah 29:11*
- *Trust in the Lord with all of your heart and lean not on your own understanding. In all your ways acknowledge Him, and He will direct your path. Proverbs 3:5–6*
- *But I trust in you, Oh Lord, you are my God; my times are in your hands. Psalm 31:14–15*

- *And we know that in all things God works for the good of those who love Him, who have been called according to His purpose. Romans 8:28*
- *Praise be to the God and Father of our Lord Jesus Christ, the Father of compassion and the God of all comfort, who comforts us in all our troubles, so that we can comfort those in trouble with the comfort we ourselves have received from God. 2 Corinthians 1:3–4*
- *Do not be anxious about anything, but in everything by prayer and petition, with thanksgiving, present your requests to God. And the peace of God, which transcends all understanding, will guard your hearts and your minds in Christ Jesus. Philippians 4:6–7*

FINAL THOUGHTS

PRAY: Lord, I praise You and worship You for all the ways I have seen You at work through my grief. Thank You that You never have and never will let me go. I am healing and still wounded by my loss. I am glued together with You by the golden scars You have used for my recovery. You have and continue to be with me and carry me on my journey. I honor You when I honor the one/s I love. Thank you for loving me as only You can. Amen

God Overcomes Loss from Death. We continue to miss your loved one/s with you. You now have gold running through your wounds, binding you closer to the LORD. We praise Him with you as you are now in a new place, we trust a better place, than when you first began this workbook.

Email us with how this workbook has impacted you. We truly want your wisdom and to know if your joy has begun to return: croy-counseling@gmail.com.

References

Breyer, T. (n.d.). *Stuck to strong* (graphic illustration). Cincinnati, OH: Unpublished.

Carter, L. PhD. & Minirth, F. M.D. (2012). *The anger workbook: An interactive guide to anger management.* Nashville, TN: Thomas Nelson.

Conrad Stoppler, M., MD. (2011). *Grief, bereavement, and mourning quiz: test your understanding.* Retrieved from:
http://www.medicinenet.com/grief_bereavement_mourning_quiz/quiz.htm

Devine, M. (2014). *The 5 stages of grief and other lies that don't help anyone.* Retrieved from:
https://www.huffingtonpost.com/megan-devine/stages-of-grief_b_4414077.html

Friedman, R. (2013). *The best grief definition you will find.* Retrieved from:
http://blog.griefrecoverymethod.com/blog/2013/06/best-grief-definition-you-will-find

Guthrie, N. (2016). *What grieving people wish you knew: About what really helps and what really hurts.* Wheaton, IL: Crossway.

The Holy Bible. New International Version (unless noted otherwise), Grand Rapids, MI: Zondervan.

Humphrey, K. M. (2009). *Counseling strategies for loss and grief.* Alexandria, VA: American Counseling Association.

Hunt, J. (2013). *Grief: Living at peace with loss*. Dallas, TX: Hope for the Heart.

Khoshaba, D., Psy.D. (2013). *About complicated bereavement disorder: when grieving worsens, rather than gets better.* Retrieved from:

https://www.psychologytoday.com/blog/get-hardy/201309/about-complicated-bereavement-disorder-0

Moore, B. (2009). *Praying God's word: Breaking free from spiritual strongholds*. Nashville, TN: B&H Publishing Group.

Nouwen, H. (1996). *The inner voice of love: A journey through anguish to freedom*. New York, NY: Image Books.

Peritz, A. (2015). *What whac-a-mole an teach us about how to fight terrorism*. Retrieved from:

http://foreignpolicy.com/2015/08/12/what-whac-a-mole-can-teach-us-about-how-to-fight-terrorism/

Sittser, J. (2004). *A grief disguised: How the soul grows through loss*. Grand Rapids, MI: Zondervan.

Stronghold. (n.d.). *Merriam-Webster Dictionary online*. Retrieved from:

https://www.merriam-webster.com/dictionary/stronghold

Transformation. (n.d.). *Merriam-Webster Dictionary online*. Retrieved from:

https://www.merriam-webster.com/dictionary/transformation

Trust. (n.d.). In *Merriam-Webster Thesaurus online*. Retrieved from:

https://www.merriam-webster.com/thesaurus/trust

WebMD. (n.d.). *Unresolved grief — topic overview*. Retrieved from:

http://www.webmd.com/a-to-z-guides/tc/unresolved-grief-topic-overview

WebMD. (2016, May 13). *Medical definition of grief*. Retrieved from:

http://www.medicinenet.com/script/main/art.asp?articlekey=24274

Wolfelt, A.D., PhD. (2003). *Understanding your grief: Ten essential touchstones for finding hope and healing your heart*. Fort Collins, CO: Companion Press.

Wolfelt, A.D., PhD. (2016). *Dispel the misconceptions about grief*. Retrieved from:

https://www.centerforloss.com/2016/02/touchstone-two-part-one-dispel-the-misconceptions-about-grief/

Wright, H.N., (n.d.). *Grief: A tangled ball of emotions*. (Graphic illustration). Retrieved from:

https://i.pinimg.com/originals/00/13/40/00134030b63fc3500a6cd1b27baeff3a.jpg

Appendix A: Resources

Books

Crossroads. (n.d.). *Healing groups: Grief.* Cincinnati, OH: Unpublished

Grief Recovery Handbook; James & Friedman
The action program for moving beyond death, divorce, and other losses

Experiencing Grief: Journeying through Grief — Book 2; Kenneth C. Haugk

Grief Recovery: Living at Peace with Loss; June Hunt

Pilgrimage Through Loss; Linda Lawrence Hunt
Pathways to strength and renewal after the death of a child

Walking with God through Pain and Suffering; Timothy Keller

On Death and Dying; Elizabeth Kubler-Ross
What the dying have to teach doctors, nurses, clergy and their own families

A Grief Observed; C.S. Lewis

You'll Get Through This; Max Lucado
Hope and help for your turbulent times

Through the Eyes of a Lion; Levi Lusko
Facing impossible pain, finding incredible power

How to Go on Living When Someone You Love Dies;
Therese Rando

Option B; Sandberg & Grant
Facing adversity, building resilience and finding joy

A Grief Disguised: How the soul grows through loss;
Jerry Sittser

I Will Carry You: The Sacred Dance of Grief and Joy;
Angie Smith

Praying the Names of God; Ann Spangler

Praying the Names of Jesus; Ann Spangler

A Place of Healing; Joni Earekson Tada
Wrestling with the mysteries of suffering, pain, and God's sovereignty

Good Grief; Granger E. Westberg

The Shack: Where tragedy confronts eternity;
William P. Young

Articles

"Find the Source of you Loneliness;" Henri Nouwen
in *The Inner Voice of Love: A Journey through Anguish to Freedom*

"Let Deep Speak to Deep;" Henri Nouwen
in *The Inner Voice of Love: Journey through Anguish to Freedom*

Hope: "The Anchor of the Soul;" Charles Stanley

"Explore Your Feelings of Loss;" Alan D. Wolfelt PhD.

The dual process model of coping with bereavement:
Stroebe & Schut
rationale and description

Websites

Adams, L.B.; A psychologist's perspective on guilt vs. regret.
http://lisabadams.com/2011/02/07/from-a-psychologists-perspective-guilt-vs-regret/

Burgo, J., Ph.D.; The difference between guilt and shame.
https://www.psychologytoday.com/us/blog/shame/201305/thedifference-between-guilt-and-shame

Kintsukuroi
http://ldsperfectday.blogspot.com/2013/12/why-word-kintsukuroi-means-so-much-to.html

Webster, B.; *Theories of grief.*
https://griefjourney.com/startjourney/for-professionals-and-caregivers/articles-for-professionals-and-caregivers/theories-of-grief/

Williams, L.; Grieving someone you didn't like (because it happens).
https://whatsyourgrief.com/grieving-someone-you-didnt-like/

Williams, L.; Guilt vs regret in grief. Retrieved from:
https://whatsyourgrief.com/guilt-vs-regret-in-grief/

Wolfelt, A.D. PhD.; Will I grieve or will I mourn?
http://griefwords.com/index.cgi?action=page&page=articles%2Fhelping36.html&site_id=7

https://whatsyourgrief.com

https://www.griefrecoverymethod.com

https://www.centerforloss.com

Appendix B: G.O.L.D. Scriptures

Chapter 1

Psalm 31:12: I am forgotten as though I were dead; I have become like broken pottery.

Isaiah 64:8 *Hebrews 4:16* *1 Thess. 5:23–24*

Romans 8:26

Chapter 2

Psalm 18:6,16: In my distress, I called to the LORD; I cried to my God for help…He reached down from on high and took hold of me; he drew me out of deep waters.

Psalm 31:9 *Isaiah 43:2* *Matthew 5:4*

Isaiah 41:10

Chapter 3

Psalm 71:20 *John 11:33* *Job 36:15*

Proverbs 3: 5–6 *Psalm 142:1–3* *Isaiah 53:3*

Psalm 42:2–7 *Malachi 3:6* *Psalm 34:18*

Chapter 4

Psalm 42:9–10: I say to God my Rock, "Why have you forgotten me? Why must I go about mourning, oppressed by the enemy?" My bones suffer mortal agony as my foes taunt me, saying to me all day long, "Where is your God?"

Job 3	James 1:14–15	Job 38:4–39
Job 7	Job 9:1-11	Job 42:2–6
Genesis 2:16–17	Job 9:16–17	Psalm 62:8
Genesis 3:1–24	Job 10	Genesis 1:31
Romans 5:12	Luke 23: 42–43	John 3:16
Proverbs 14:30	Matthew 19:14	Romans 8:28
Obadiah 3:3	Psalms 147:4	Mark 3:5
Psalm 38:4	Titus 3:5	John 10:10a
John 8:32	Matthew 6:34	
Job 38:1		

Chapter 5

Matthew 5:4: Blessed are those who mourn for they shall be comforted.

Psalm 10:17	Romans 8:31	Hebrews 12:11
Proverbs 10:7	John 14:27	

Chapter 6

2 Corinthians 10:3-4: For though we live in the world, we do not wage war as the world does. The weapons we fight with are not the weapons of the world. On the contrary, they have divine power to demolish strongholds

Ephesians 4:26–27	Romans 8:1	1 Peter 2:1
Hebrews 6:18-19	Proverbs 3:5–6	1 Peter 5:7
Psalm 18:2	2 Corinthians 7:10	1 Corinthians 10:13
1 Thess. 5:16–18	1 John 3:20	2 Corinthians 4:8–9

Chapter 7

Lamentations 3:55–57: I called on your name, Lord, from the depths of the pit. You heard my plea: "Do not close your ears to my cry for relief." You came near when I called you, and you said, "Do not fear."

Matthew 6:9–13	Psalm 68:5	2 Corinthians 2:10–11a
2 Corinthians 6:18	Ephesians 4:30–32	2 Corinthians 7:10
Mark 11:25	1 John 1:9	Matthew 6:14–15
Ezekiel 28:2	Proverbs 24:16	Psalm 103:12
Job 12:13	Psalm 91:4	Romans 2:4
Matthew 11:29	Colossians 3:13	1 John 2:12
John 8:3-11		

Chapter 8

Colossians 1:16–17: For in him all things were created: things in heaven and on earth, visible and invisible, whether thrones or powers or rulers or authorities; all things have been created through him and for him. He is before all things, **and in him all things hold together.**

Lamentation 3:19–26	Revelation 22:13	Philippians 4:13
Matthew 1:22–23	Philippians 2:9–11	John 11:25–26
John 8:12	Proverbs 3:5	Galatians 2:20
John 6:48–51	2 Corinthians 12:7–10	Psalm 139:7–10
Isaiah 9:6	Philippians 4:19	2 Corinthians 4:7-9
John 1:14	2 Corinthians 9:8	Revelation 22:16
Ephesians 1:10		

Chapter 9

Psalm 51:10: Create in me a pure heart, O God, and renew a steadfast spirit within me.

Ecclesiastes 3:1	Proverbs 16:3	Matthew 25:34
Ephesians 2:10	Romans 12:2	Revelation 21:4
James 4:7	Ephesians 1:19	Psalm 96
Psalm 139:11–12	Matthew 6:33	Romans 5:3–5
Philippians 4:6	Colossians 3:12	2 Peter 1:3

Chapter 10

Psalm 145:7: Everyone will share the story of your wonderful goodness; they will sing with joy about your righteousness.

Philippians 4:8	Proverbs 3:5-6	Romans 8:28
Jeremiah 29:11	Psalm 31:14-15	2 Corinthians 1:3-4
Philippians 4:6-7	Galatians 5:22	

About the Authors

Cinny Roy is a licensed professional clinical counselor as well as the founder and director emeritus of the Eve Center (evecenter.org). She is the author of *From Clouds to Concrete: Starting & Leading a Christian Nonprofit*. Working on G.O.L.D. with this team has been an honor as together they desire to see men and women recover from debilitating grief. Cinny lives and works in Cincinnati, Ohio.

Tambra Breyer recently received her Master of Ministry degree through Cedarville University. She is a volunteer peer counselor at the Eve Center as well as the Prayer and Care Ministry deacon at her church in Springboro, Ohio. Her desire to help those stuck in grief stems from the devastating loss of her daughter Sydney. The opportunity to contribute to the G.O.L.D. curriculum has brought beauty from ashes in a way that only God can. To Him be the glory.

Patsy Andow-Plum is an Ohio licensed professional counselor specializing in grief and loss among adults. As a registered architect, she expresses herself through creative experiences like painting, singing, piano playing and ballroom dancing. On great weather days, you will probably find her out in the woods exploring God's creation or riding on the motorcycle with her husband.

Kathy D. Schibler, APRN, RN, has been a nurse practitioner in primary care for over 20 years. Now retired, she is a volunteer peer counselor at the Eve Center for Women located in Cincinnati, Ohio. She has a special interest in walking along side women experiencing grief. It has been my pleasure to be a part of this team writing this G.O.L.D. curriculum and giving praise to God.

www.ingramcontent.com/pod-product-compliance
Lightning Source LLC
Chambersburg PA
CBHW070200100426
42743CB00013B/2984